DevOps ICU:
Improve
Processes and
Results by
Correctly
Integrating UX

*A Guide for Product, Project, and Engineering Leaders
and Workers*

Debbie Levitt

TABLE OF CONTENTS

DEVOPS ICU: IMPROVE PROCESSES AND RESULTS BY CORRECTLY INTEGRATING UX
A Guide for Product, Project, and Engineering Leaders and Workers

Book v1.0

Edited by Jill Ivey www.jilletante.com

Cover designed Debbie Levitt.

Ptype and **The Four Horsemen of Bad UX** are registered trademarks of Brass Flowers Inc. **DevOps ICU** and **the DevOps ICU logo** are trademarks (registration in progress) of Brass Flowers Inc.

This book is a work of fiction. Names, characters, places, and incidents either are products of the author's imagination or are used fictitiously. Any resemblance to actual persons, living or dead, events, or locales is entirely coincidental.

Debbie Levitt
Visit my website at www.DebbieLevitt.com

Printed in the United States of America

First Edition/Printing: April 2019
Debbie Levitt (self-published)

ISBN 9781092909167

This book is dedicated to my boyfriend, who is an amazing and beautiful person with endless empathy.
He listened to this what seemed like hundreds of times. He's helpful, supportive, and always my hero.
I'm grateful for him (roughly) 500 times a day.
I love you, teammate!

INTRODUCTION

In case anyone isn't familiar with the term "ICU," it's the Intensive Care Unit—the part of a hospital giving care and treatment to the most critical of patients. The ICU is also metaphorically where you might find your DevOps.

I'm your DevOps ICU "doctor," Debbie Levitt. I've been a UX strategist, designer, and consultant since the mid-90s. My full-service UX and product design agency, Ptype [pty.pe]—short for prototype—takes on small and large UX projects, and also helps companies build or improve UX teams, including deciding where UX belongs in an organization, hiring, onboarding, training, processes, tools, and getting departments on the same page.

Clients (independently) have given me a nickname: "Mary Poppins." I fly in, fix everything, sing a few songs, and fly away to where I'm needed next... though it's best when UX specialists stay on a project to collaborate with Engineering and Product, and continue the learn–build–test cycle.

As a "serial contractor" who lived in the Bay Area, California for most of the 2010's, I've influenced interfaces at Sony, Wells Fargo, Constant Contact, Macys.com, Oracle, and a variety of Silicon Valley startups. I'm also a speaker and trainer, presenting at conferences and events including eBay's Developer Conference, PayPal's Developer Conference, UXPA, WeAreDevelopers, and many regional Agile, Lean, and DevOps events. I'm an O'Reilly published author and one of few instructors on the planet recommended by Axure.

Outside of UX work, and sometimes during UX work, I enjoy singing symphonic prog-goth metal, opera, and new wave. I'm now a digital nomad splitting my time between the USA and rural Italy. Come visit Italy and we'll make it a business trip.

DEVOPS ICU

This book is the short version of my newest training program, "DevOps ICU." It teaches non-UX roles how to measurably improve DevOps results by correctly integrating UX practitioners and processes. Learn more at DevOpsICU.com.

I was compelled to write the training program (and now this book) after years working in companies of all sizes around San Francisco and Silicon Valley. I spoke to colleagues who worked elsewhere, connected with people in Engineering and Product, and there was a clear pattern: **People don't understand UX and they're not sure how it works into their organizations.**

UX professionals think they need to evangelize themselves, even adding "UX evangelism" as an activity required at certain jobs! But evangelism just makes UX workers look weird; no other team or department is holding meetings about how awesome they are and how important they can be.

You've probably had conflicts with UX practitioners. They don't seem Lean or Agile—in fact, they're throwing off your Agile train so badly you want to throw them under it! They're killing ideas, timelines, and budgets. Their work looks easy, why can't you just do it yourselves? UX seems like a black box disappearing for weeks or months and then just telling us what to build. Where are the communication and collaboration?

UX practitioners are keenly aware of these conflicts and how they are seen as the problem. Non-UX roles have many misunderstandings and myths about UX including these issues:

- Agile methodologies often don't mention UX at all, as if the people designing what Engineering will build are not important or necessary.
- Everybody thinks UX is just wireframes and "anybody can draw boxes on a page," but it's far from that.
- UX isn't formalized and doesn't have defined processes or approaches; it's whatever the designer "feels like." False!
- Companies select the wrong people for a job that HR and hiring managers don't understand. They think these roles require artists, but UX is not an art job.
- Teams are sure they don't need UX or can't afford it, often without knowing what UX work and tools actually cost.
- Product managers often want to "do UX work" before or during a project. However, they don't realize that what they are doing isn't really UX.

- Developers I meet at conferences either don't know what UX is or tell me, "Yeah, you're the people who A/B test things after we release them!" That's too late for user testing. Wouldn't they like to know before they code that what they're working on has been validated as being a good product or feature for customers? (Oh, they think that sounds really good!)

You'll learn to dispel these UX myths, misunderstandings, and more in our time together. Thanks for joining me in helping to get DevOps out of the ICU.

Book notes:

- When I'm talking about teams or departments, I will capitalize words like, "Product," "Creative," or "Engineering," so that this isn't confused with "the product" we're building or someone who is "creative."
- I often use "we" or "our" to talk about UX since it's the industry in which I work.

Take the polls!

Throughout the book, you'll find polls you can take from your phone or computer. I encourage you to join in—each question is fast and worth thinking about!

To start, visit menti.com and use code 187448 and answer the first three questions so I can get to know my readers and further improve DevOps ICU.

Q1: In which area do you work?

Q2: These are some of the complaints I hear most about UX. Which ones do you believe?

Q3: How does your team work with UX now?

Thanks!

REDEFINING DEVOPS

Your customer only cares about your user experience.

At many companies, Engineering is fed by other teams. Blueprints, ideas, designs, and concepts come from somebody who creates layouts, flows, and the ways customers interact with the system. These non-engineering individuals and teams are collaborators throughout the software development process. Engineering doesn't operate in a vacuum.

Too many companies are excluding or circumventing UX because they see it excluded from Agile maps, infographics, books, how-tos, and trainings. They assume that UX workers are time and budget wasters or that UX is *just wireframes* and anybody can draw boxes on a page.

These assumptions are incorrect. Expert UX architects research, design, test, and iterate on everything between someone saying, "I have an idea!" and, "Let's get it to programmers to be built."

DevOps is about so much more than how developers connect with IT, how infrastructure is managed, and how frameworks can be improved. It's about recognizing how many teams are truly involved in the software development process, how intertwined their roles and work are, and finding better ways to make sure everybody is at the table.

Developers and engineering architects want to be involved when the Product and Creative teams are designing the software or system, but they perceive UX to be a black box. Product, UX, and Creative teams want to stay involved during engineering's processes, yet so many methodologies exclude them. This doesn't fit in the current definition of DevOps. These are old silos that we need to break down.

WHO DESIGNED THIS PRODUCT?

Your customer only perceives your user experience. That's it and that's all they care about. They don't see 1000 developers or whether you were Agile, Waterfall, or Lean.

Remember: you're also a user, a customer of many products and systems. The software and systems you use have competitors. What made you select and use the tools, software, apps, or systems you chose? When you use a system you don't like, are you thinking, "Man, how many sprints did they spend on *that*?" Probably not.

When something doesn't work the way you expected it to, you're probably thinking, "Who built this junk?"

That's a good question.

Who designed this product? Who researched with users like you to learn your habits, motivations, and needs, and then design for those? Was this tested on people like you before it was unleashed on the public? The product might have been "designed" by a product owner who described a feature to developers. The business analyst may have made some layouts. A visual designer who says they can do wireframes might have "designed" it. The CEO might have told everybody what they wanted it to look like. But did those really work for you, the customer?

You'll often hear that good UX is invisible or the customer doesn't perceive the work that went into UX when it's good. But people certainly notice when it's bad. How many times have you wished to go back to the old version of something? How many times did that app update change something that was important to you, making the app harder to use?

Most of us have seen the video of the bridge that waves and wobbles until it crumbles. We always remember the bridges that famously failed. But we don't even think about bridges that are soundly constructed. That's what great UX is like. The company doing great UX work will have the customers. You can market the heck out of a crappy product but people are smarter than that. They won't stick with it.

You have to be user-centric because your customers are user-centric. Your customers only care about themselves. What do they want or need? How does this product work for them? That's all they care about: they just want it to work—and it should just work the way they expect it to work. That means we need experts to get inside our customers' heads, talk to them, and know what they expect.

And even though I'm talking about customers, plural, it's important to think also about individual needs. You can't design one product and expect it to be a perfect fit for everyone, but you need to know that you're meeting the needs of as many individual customers as possible, in a unified way. Which means your experts have to be amazing at designing for a lot of different needs at the same time into what might be only one product.

THE VALUE OF THE UX SPECIALTY

Throughout this book, we'll look at examples in which companies put themselves at risk by giving the UX tasks to wrong people, fail when the product doesn't match real user needs and pain points, and stumble when they "just ship" something that misses the mark. All of these problems result in customer dissatisfaction.

But how can we know ahead of time that taking these risks might end up in failure? This is where UX shines. Using our own flavor of the research, build, test, and iterate cycle, UX pros can know ahead of time where a product or feature is likely to create frustration, confusion, or disappointment.

People often imagine that UX design is just drawing boxes on a page. That's like saying programming is writing letters on a screen. When UX practitioners are creating wireframes or prototypes, they're not designing whatever they like. They are informed by UX research, the design concepts are validated or invalidated in UX testing, and flaws can then be fixed during an iteration period. This is all before Engineering writes a line of code.

UX is a specialized area in which practitioners research, organize, design, test, and iterate using methods and approaches we'll learn more about in our time together. Adding UX experts and their tasks to internal processes brings benefits, including:

- **Huge time and money savings for Engineering.** Build it once and build it right the first time because UX is providing the blueprints. No more guessing at how this should lay out or work, no more endless rebuilds because *someone changed their mind.*
- **Lower costs for customer service and social media managers.** Fewer problems with the product and fewer areas that are confusing or hard to use mean customers will be better able to accomplish their own tasks, leading to less load on support reps and fewer ugly social media complaints that require rapid response.
- **Happier (and more!) word-of-mouth.** Your Net Promoter Score is likely to go up, people will want to recommend a product they love, and influencers may have more positive things to say about you.

- **Better customer retention.** Even with lots of slick marketing, discounts, and promises, a poor product will still bleed customers.
- **Better employee retention.** People might stick around more if they are building something that makes customers happy. Jobs are more rewarding and morale is higher when there are fewer complaints coming in from customers.
- **Higher stock price.** Nobody can guarantee this, but you can research companies that had famous, public UX fails and how their stocks suffered afterwards.
- **More conversions on your site or in your app.** Great user experience makes it easier for customers to understand your product, easier for them to select products or services, and easier to complete that purchase.
- **Broadened customer base.** You might currently be excluding differently-abled customers because you haven't invested in making your product accessible. Instead, build for all possible target customers, not just some. For those who care about the bottom line and aren't swayed by the usual, "Do the right thing," argument, meeting and exceeding accessibility standards can keep you from getting sued.

That's the short version. We'll unpack these ideas and more throughout the book.

WHO IS FOCUSED ON PRODUCT QUALITY AND THE VOICE OF THE CUSTOMER?

A March 2018 article by John Steven boils down the key differences between Agile, CI/CD, and DevOps. [https://www.synopsys.com/blogs/software-security/agile-cicd-devops-glossary/] He summarizes these differences as follows:

- Agile focuses on processes, highlighting change, while accelerating delivery.
- CI/CD focuses on software-defined life cycles, highlighting tools that emphasize automation.
- DevOps focuses on culture, highlighting roles that emphasize responsiveness.

Then who's focused on the product and building what customers really need? Who is gathering feedback from the customer and interpreting it? Who's feeding project, product, or portfolio with data and informed suggestions on what we should build or change?

That's the role UX plays and why user experience professionals must be brought more fully into the software development universe. In addition to doing specialty research and product design work, UX focuses on areas that might not be getting much Engineering attention right now.

UX IS ALIGNED WITH DEVOPS GOALS AND DESIRED RESULTS

Think of DevOps like a restaurant. A restaurant experience is about so much more than what came out of the kitchen. If the cooks don't work well together or get things done efficiently, the restaurant can fail. If the kitchen cooks bad tasting stuff, the restaurant can fail. If the waiters do a bad job taking orders or bringing out food, the restaurant can fail. If the cooks are skilled at cooking but they start with cheap and bad ingredients, the restaurant can fail. If the food is good but the place is dirty, the restaurant can fail. If the people in the kitchen have a good culture and good efficiency, the restaurant can still fail.

The kitchen doesn't operate as a silo. There are too many moving pieces, team players, and necessary collaborations. When a customer uses our software, system, website, or app, any one or more things going wrong can create customer dissatisfaction even if measurements of efficiency, productivity, agility, or velocity were great.

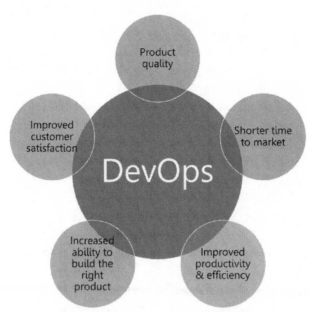

Figure 1: Desired DevOps results include product quality, shorter time to market, improved productivity and efficiency, increased ability to build the right product, and improved customer satisfaction.

UX is driven by some of the same results DevOps wants. We're problem finders, problem solvers, product designers, and customer advocates, driven by product quality and customer needs. We care about our teams working efficiently and getting engaging, fantastic, easy-to-learn, easy-to-use, tell-your-friends-it's-great products to market as fast as possible.

Enhancing this relationship saves time, money, and sanity.

We want the DevOps ICU hospital bed to be empty because the patient recovered and is better than ever. If your DevOps needs critical care and treatment, UX can't fix everything. But perhaps you'd be surprised how much UX can improve.

Everything UX does is aligned with DevOps and its goals. Working more closely with UX, improving collaboration, and finding the right ways to incorporate UX practitioners and processes into your software development methodologies will improve product quality, time to market, productivity and efficiency, your ability to build the right product, and increased customer satisfaction... all while saving you money and increasing worker happiness along the way.

WHERE UX FITS INTO PROCESSES

Imagine the glorious experience of building the right product for the customer... once.

f your company or team doesn't include a UX practitioner or process, your world probably looks like this:

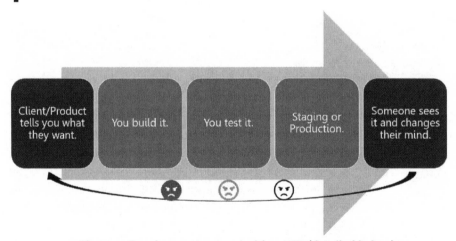

Figure 2: Development process without UX (detailed below).

1. The "Client" tells Engineering what they want. This might be a product manager, CEO, external client, or person with the vision for the product or feature.
2. Dev builds it.
3. QA tests it.
4. The code goes to staging or production.

5.   The person with the initial vision says, "Ya know, now that I see it, it's not really what I want. Let's make some changes."
6.   Breathe deeply and start the process again. *What do they want now?*
7.   You rebuild, you retest, you get your code on a server, you hope, and cross every finger you have.
8.   After repeated cycles, you eventually release something live and hope that customers like it.

This sounds pretty awful. Can this still be considered Agile? Sounds more like Anguish.

If you correctly integrate UX into your processes, your happier life looks more like this:

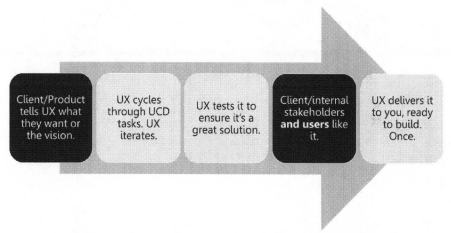

Figure 3: Development process including UX (detailed below).

1.   That person with the vision gives the UX practitioner ideas, features, or stories.
2.   UX cycles through UCD tasks. UX iterates to create the best execution.
3.   UX tests their wireframed or prototyped designs to ensure it's a great solution.
4.   After testing validates the design, everybody should be on the same page. The client and/or internal stakeholders like it. It works well for the user. It's ready to be sent to Engineering.
5.   UX delivers it to Engineering, ready to build. Once.

6. If the client wants to change their mind, they come back to UX, not to Engineering. UX runs interference by keeping all of the design tasks and changes inside of its own processes.

Figure 4: Ahhhh, Engineering might only need to build this once!

The goal is for you to build a fantastic, vetted product ONCE. Can you smell that? That's the sweet smell of not having to keep rebuilding the same thing over and over because someone keeps changing their mind.

WHERE UX FITS INTO AN ORGANIZATION

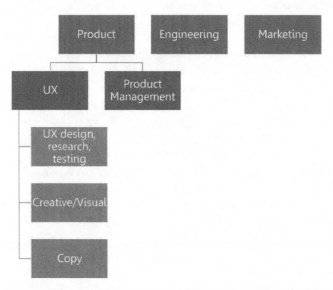

Figure 5: Suggested UX placement in org chart (detailed below).

Because so many people misunderstand UX, I've seen it thrown into just about every area of an organization you can imagine.

I've seen UX answer to Marketing. When we disagree with Marketing, which is often, guess who loses. UX isn't about the marketing of a product or how do we sell people what the business wants to build. It's about product-market fit, designing something that truly meets users' researched and validated needs. Marketing often asks, "Will you buy this?" or wonders internally how will we sell things to people, whether or not people really want them. UX asks, "How can we improve this so that it's better, faster, or easier for the customer?"

I've seen UX answer to Engineering. Despite Agile being a cyclical process that sometimes doubles back on itself, Engineering expected our processes to be more concrete and easier to timebox and predict. This creates a lot of natural conflict, which means UX as a subset of Engineering is a poor match.

I've seen UX answer to Creative, normally an artist acting as Creative Director or a VP of Design. The problem there tends to be that artists expect everybody under them to be artists. You end up with jobs with UX titles that require art education, art talent, art technique, sometimes even art sub-specialties like illustration. UX teams run by artists have tended to over focus on the aesthetics of the interface rather than all of the other elements a UX expert is normally focused on primarily. I've seen this in Fortune 100 companies; it's a common mistake, but one we need to clean up.

I've even seen heads of Design who are not familiar with the full User-Centered Design process and believe that skipping most of UX's most important tasks is just fine. Artists managing UX seems natural, but is really a mismatch.

I've seen the most success where UX is its own department with its own head, director, and/or VP. UX would then ultimately answer organizationally at a very high level to Product since at our core, UX practitioners are product designers. However, UX still needs autonomy since Product very often is excited about their roadmap and ideas; UX can suffer when too much is dictated or prescribed by Product.

That means that based on where I have seen the most UX success, UX would be on the same level as Product Management but has its own leadership. UX does not answer to product managers. Both departments answer to someone responsible for the whole arc or spectrum of Product. Whether you are already working with UX or looking to add them to your company or processes, consider this approach.

Additionally, the best organizational approach is for visual design or graphic design and copy to be part of the UX department. At the very least, these people collaborate with UX architects. In a future chapter, you will learn how these roles are subsets of UX and part of our process.

Some companies put visual design under Marketing since Marketing needs lots of graphics created and someone to be the brand steward. A larger company might have visual design staff in both departments, some working on UX and some working on marketing. If your company is smaller, visual design can be under UX and still work with Marketing on their design needs.

WAVES OF COLLABORATION

Engineering often wants to know when UX practitioners will ask their opinions on what is being designed. UX must collaborate with Engineering early, before UX tasks begin, to learn boundaries, limitations, and technologies. What I call "waves of collaboration" explain when UX will show different teammates their work and listen to feedback on the concepts and designs.

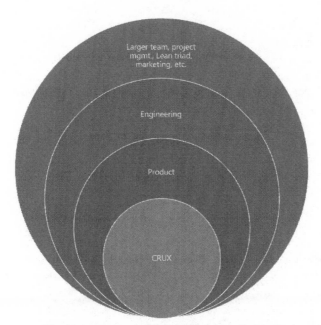

Figure 6: Waves of collaboration (detailed below).

The first set of collaborators on a project is what we call CRUX—that's a combination of "creative" and "UX." That means your UX workers, your visual designers, and your copywriters are one collaborative team. UX often does some UX tasks and then checks in with visual designers and copy. It's common for Slack or other chat apps to have a private room just for CRUX.

CRUX is a great name for our sub-team since we really are the core of how the product, system, app, or software ends up.

If the designs are passing internal review, UX will then present the work to the product manager. It's Product's turn to check that they feel it matches vision, requirements, user stories, and other relevant elements. There might also be a private chat room just for CRUX and Product, often just called "Product." If Product feels something doesn't match the vision or intention, or a story was missed, UX has the chance to iterate before anybody else has seen the work-in-progress.

Moving on from there, UX will then present the work to Engineering. This is the point at which they'll ask questions about the feasibility of their design so far. Can you do this? Can you do it with the time, budget, and resources we have? Do we need APIs written? Would these concepts force changes to back-end systems the company might not be ready to make? As these are important questions and can change the direction of the design, UX needs to be asking them before anything is sent to user testing or is considered finalized.

If all is still going well, UX might run this by the larger team, which might include more people from the Agile train, a Lean Triad, project managers, marketing (if they are looking for an early peek at what might be built), and other stakeholders.

Note that at each point of collaboration, UX presents its own work. Do not let Product, Engineering, or anyone else present it. There are often follow-up or challenge questions about this work, and your UX teammate is the best and most qualified person to answer them. Additionally, if people start offering ideas for how the product should designed differently, it's best for UX to field those ideas, consider whether the ideas are a match to the target audiences, and decide if they will be included or not. The risk in having non-UX roles field these questions is that those folks might hear these ideas and promise that they will be included. Not all ideas will be included, and the best way to make sure you don't make promises you can't keep is to have UX in the room fielding their own questions.

After everybody is on board, the designs, concepts, wireframes, or prototypes can then go through user testing so we can find and iterate on flaws.

Once the UX designs are considered final or close to final, a visual designer will add their touch. The CRUX collaboration continues. UX typically checks the artist's work to make sure that the UX design is intact and hasn't been significantly changed by the visual designer. Some companies want to do the visual design while the UX design work is being done, but we'll cover later why this isn't always the best idea.

I once passed my work to a visual designer, who then sent back something completely different from what I designed. When I asked her why she had changed what I did, her response was, "Oh... was what you designed deliberate?"

Yes, it's all deliberate. UX isn't about whims. It's not, "Aw, I just put that there," or, "Gee, this would look nice," or even, "I like this!" UX practitioners often must explain their designs to their own co-workers, especially if there are departmental design reviews. We have to be able to explain everything we've designed and why it's the best choice for our customer. That means everything we do is deliberate and without ego. If your UX practitioner is high ego... they might want to shift career paths.

All UX specialists should to be able to say: [this idea or design] works for [these personas] for [these reasons].

"SIMPLE SYSTEMS AND INTERNAL CUSTOMERS DON'T NEED UX"

Some declare that "simple systems" and products built for co-workers don't need UX practitioners or tasks. Who told you they didn't? The developer? Product manager?

The only opinions that matter are the customers'. Did a UX expert run research or testing with your real or potential customers and find that they are happy with your product?

I've heard from multiple people that their organization doesn't want to invest in or include UX because, "the product is shallow," "the screens are simple with few choices," or, "it's for internal workers, not outside paying customers." Let's break down these arguments.

The product is shallow or the screens are fairly simple with few choices. You should still be working with UX to design and test products. What you perceive as simplicity might not be simplicity to our users. Put on your empathy hat and imagine that not everybody has the knowledge, understanding, experience, or familiarity you have with this system.

Having only a few choices doesn't mean that content and information are presented well. It doesn't mean those choices are located in places on the screen that are easy to find without confusion. Remember ancient times when we accidentally clicked "reset" when we meant to hit "submit" at the end of an online form? Those were two simple choices yet we clicked the wrong one with some frequency. Don't assume that having few choices means that the layouts or processes really work for customers.

Our customers are internal so we don't really need to bother with UX design. I've heard this from so many industries from insurance to the US government. If you are confident in that, please walk over to your co-workers, the people who will use this system, and tell them out loud that you don't care if they have an easy time using this or not. You don't care if processes are long, confusing, slow, difficult, and frustrating. You're not going to ask them what they need or how this could be better. You're not going to watch them use it to test for usability issues and improve the interactivity.

You are affecting someone's ability to do their job. You agonize over your and your team's productivity, efficiency, ROI, etc. but you are essentially saying that you don't care if someone else's productivity and efficiency are harmed by your lack of care about your system's UX.

How about your co-workers who make commission based on the products or services they sell from these systems? What about co-workers with quotas for how many customers they need to serve, tickets they need to reply to, or situations they need to handle with this system? You don't care if you are hurting their ability to meet or beat quotas?

I hear, "Well, the systems *we* use aren't easy so why should we make someone else's system easier??" or, "They'll just have to learn whatever we build." If you ever think or say things like this, you need to put that empathy hat on. Your difficulties at your job aren't a license to unleash negativity on someone else.

Start a ball rolling of empathy and concern for how efficient, happy, and productive we can make other people. You might find that empathy and good design are contagious, you feel rewarded by making jobs and lives easier for your co-workers, and that good karma might circle its way back to you and what you need at your job.

More importantly, happier employees will be more productive.

So... how does UX do it?

WHAT IS UX?

I was once in a kickoff meeting with a cross-functional team. We went over the high-level version of what our project would be and we all introduced ourselves. As the meeting was winding down, someone asked, "Who is going to design this thing?" Quickly, the engineering lead said he guessed that he would design it.

I asked if anybody knew what my job is or what UX is? Everybody said, "No." A project manager, a product manager, an engineering lead, a developer, and a QA engineer. Nobody in the room knew what I did. They thought they were going to design the product themselves.

This was at a company that is on both the American and global Fortune 500 lists. These were experienced, senior-level practitioners!

It's no longer OK for workers, leaders, managers, or executives anywhere in the product and software development process not to know what UX is or what practitioners do. You're going to learn that now, and on behalf of every UX worker on the planet, thank you for reading this book.

What is UX? User Experience (UX) is the more scientific, psychological, and problem-solving side of product, experience, and service design. Key goals include:

- Happier, more loyal customers.
- Ease of learning and use.
- Shorter, more intuitive processes.
- Accessibility for people with mobility, vision, hearing, cognitive, or other issues.

Let's look at each of these goals individually.

HAPPIER, MORE LOYAL CUSTOMERS

Nobody wants unhappy customers who are ready to jump ship or have already started cancelling their accounts with you so they can sign up with your competitors.

When UX researches who customers are, what their needs and pain points are, and what they are likely to do, your company can have a better idea of what you should (and shouldn't) design and build for them.

It's hard to make someone happy when you don't know or understand what they want. Think back to an unsuccessful romantic relationship you had. (Sorry for the bad memories!) There's a good chance that, in one way or another, it ended because one of you was unhappy or wasn't having your needs met. So if you don't want your customers to break up with you, you have to bring in experts who will research them, get to know them, and include them in many steps of the process so their needs and voices are always heard and considered.

EASE OF LEARNING AND USE

"I can't wait to read the user manual for my new tech device," said almost no one, ever. And especially no one recently, as most new devices no longer come with manuals.

When products without manuals started becoming standard practice, people thought companies were being cheap, trying to save money on paper and printing by including a CD with a PDF manual on it... or eventually no manual in any form. But companies know now that people just don't read the manual.

Frustrated support reps and software engineers often hear about users' problems and want to reply, "RTFM" (that's "read the *bleeping* manual"). But a product that is easy to learn and easy to use shouldn't need a manual. Did you need a manual for the last smartphone you bought? Or did you charge it up, turn it on, and *it just worked*?

You want your customers to use your product or feature and feel like *it just works*. No tutorials, no tooltips, no instructional text, no manuals, or how-tos. These all signal to customers that you know your product is not easy to learn or use or you assume the customer won't figure it out, so you'll just lecture the customer a bit on what to do.

You hate when websites do this to you. You hate when products are hard to learn or use. To avoid passing along the same frustrations, UX work is irreplaceable here.

SHORTER, MORE INTUITIVE PROCESSES

How many steps or clicks should something take? You might be thinking, "One," but the correct answer is, "As few as possible." An entire process often can't be finished in a single click or tap, but a great UX practitioner should be able to design an interface that feels (or is) quick and intuitive to use.

If you're not sure how important this is, you'll think about this paragraph next time you are filling out an online form that wants three times the amount of information you were hoping to give the company. How about online job applications? Nothing short about those.

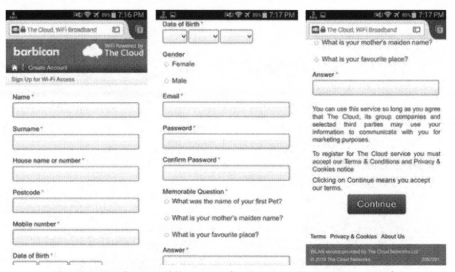

Figure 7: One long mobile screen (broken into three screen shots). 14 mandatory fields to get free Wi-Fi in a concert hall.

The concert venue in the screen shots above didn't care about shorter and more user-friendly processes when someone in the marketing department decided that "free Wi-Fi" was a great opportunity to force everybody to give up a mountain of personal information. In case you can't read the fields, they are asking for your first and last name, full home address, mobile number, birthday, gender, and email address. They also require you to create a login with password, and answer the same security question that might unlock your online banking. Plus you agree that all of this company's partners can market to you.

Free Wi-Fi simply isn't that valuable. I'll just stay on my data plan, thanks.

The next time you are going through some long, awful online process or form and you complain that the company disrespected or wasted your time, you're really saying, "I wish a UX expert had spent time designing this form for the minimal amount of time I'd like to spend on it."

ACCESSIBILITY IS FOR EVERYONE

At an American football game in late 2016, two teams decided to get creative with their uniforms, putting one team in all red and one team in all green. (Apologies to people on eReaders showing both images in greyscale, though that also proves the point!)

Figure 8: A still from a 2016 American football game featuring special uniforms.

The image below uses a filter to simulate how the game looked to people who are colorblind. Many people, including former NFL players, tweeted that they had no idea what was going on. Helmet logos would have been very small on the TV broadcast and therefore unhelpful on some of the wider camera shots.

Figure 9: The same football game with a filter applied to simulate red-green color blindness. This now appears to be the moderately pewter team versus. the slightly-brown-pewter team.

You may have thought that UX practitioners just need a few hours to draw boxes on a page, but part of our process is to take differently-abled people into consideration when designing interfaces.

There are many people who can be categorized as "disabled." It's a group that most of us will eventually end up in since as we age, we are likely to have vision, hearing, mobility, cognitive, or other issues. An online job description listed the following as some of the conditions that would qualify as "disabled" (their list and wording, not mine):

- Blindness
- Deafness
- Cancer
- Diabetes
- Epilepsy
- Autism
- Cerebral palsy
- HIV/AIDS
- Schizophrenia
- Muscular dystrophy
- Bipolar disorder
- Major depression

- Multiple sclerosis (MS)
- Missing limbs or partially missing limbs
- Post-traumatic stress disorder (PTSD)
- Obsessive compulsive disorder
- Impairments requiring the use of a wheelchair
- Intellectual disability

How many of these describe you? How many of these describe your family, friends, and co-workers? All of these can affect how someone uses digital interfaces: smartphones, tablets, computers, laptops, smart watches, car screens (replacing dashboards), smart thermostats, and smart devices.

Not only is accessibility the law in some countries, but also when you make a site better for those with motion, hearing, vision, cognitive, and other issues, you make it better for everybody. Accessibility makes interfaces better and easier to use for all humans.

In the USA, accessibility became part of the Americans with Disabilities Act as of January 2018. So, Americans: if you're not motivated by doing what's right for humans, then at least consider that violating the ADA can get you sued.

THE USER-CENTERED DESIGN PROCESS

When Product has a good idea of what solution goes with their vision, feature, or idea, it can feel efficient to just convey that to developers and have them start building. But without UX's User-Centered Design process (UCD), you might not be putting the user first or building the right thing for your customers.

Just like software dev has processes like Agile, UX has one key approach most companies and practitioners use, User-Centered Design. This can be a long process that takes time, or sometimes we're doing pieces of this and can move more quickly.

Let's take a short look at each step of the UCD process.

Figure 10: The User-Centered Design process.

Task Set 1 – Requirements and Audits

When UX first gets project requirement information, it's important to start collaborating right away. UX should *not* find out later that they have designed something that can't be built. Among the early project discovery work, UX should work with Engineering to learn more about the technologies being used, any boundaries or limitations, what services or APIs are in place, and where Engineering might have to write new ones.

Task Set 2 – User and Competitor Research

User research is an important component of what UX does. It's not User-Centered Design without users! Statistics and quantitative data are great, but there is no substitute for interviewing users, deeply understanding them, and getting qualitative data. UX wants to know the "why" and not just the "what."

Many companies make the mistake of saying that they sell to everybody, but it's usually not really everybody. Everyone has sweet spots of who the best or most likely customers are.

Personas are archetypes of our target customers. Based on interviews with users, we aggregate what we learn and boil everybody down to six or fewer personas. We give them names and find them photos. We look at who they are: What motivates them? What are their needs, frustrations, or habits? How do they currently perform tasks related to what your company offers, and what are their workarounds? Where are opportunities for our company, product, or service?

"Community Carrie"
Female, age 65

iStock #21609239

"The more we engage with others, the less we'll think about ourselves. That's my motto for life and my [disease] journey."

About Carrie:
- Carrie was diagnosed 2 years ago.
- She is retired and lives in the suburbs with her husband. They are empty nesters.
- Carrie stays pretty fit. In addition to gardening, she rides her bike a few times a week. She just joined a [disease-focused exercise] group.
- She enjoys technology. She has a Mac computer and iPhone. She got a FitBit about 18 months ago.
- She found a [disease] community on FitBit and has made new friends around the USA. They watch each other's progress.
- She added these people on Facebook. She wants to feel close to and involved with them. Carrie likes to see their comments when she posts about her journey.

Needs and Frustrations:
- Carrie doesn't mind a bit of journaling about her symptoms and experience. She'll do some manual entry into her apps. But she really wishes that her devices and apps could track so much more.
- She would like her apps to give her better data and personalized ideas. Like, "Hey, it's a great day to do some gardening. Get outside!"

Motivated by Connection With Others:
- Carrie does her best when she knows other people are "watching." That could mean FitBit friends checking what activities she has done or Facebook friends looking to see what she's up to.
- She has a competitive spirit and wants to see herself doing well on the app leaderboards.

Figure 11: Example of a persona.

Without revealing any specifics, we did this persona for a foundation looking to learn more about how people with a certain disease used fitness wearables. We interviewed 20 people diagnosed in the last few years and boiled everybody down to three personas.

The best use of personas within your organization would be to include them *everywhere*. Product imagines features based on personas (and good data). UX designs based on personas. QA tests while imagining they are these personas. Marketing can add their demographic and other details, but they should consider, too, how brand voice, social media, and advertising speak to the personas.

User stories are written from the perspective of the personas.

- *As Carrie, I can share my disease progress and changes so that I can get support from my community.*
  OR...
- *As a user motivated by social connection, I want to share my disease progress so that I can feel supported.*

When considering features and processes for customers, use empathy and method acting to put yourself in the persona's world. *I'm Sally the housewife, juggling a baby and my iPhone. How will I use this? When will I use this? Will I be able to use this at all?* What does Sally need, want, or expect in this moment?

This helps everybody get away from, "Well, I like it this way." How nice for you! We've all heard, "The CEO likes it this way." In those cases, UX should go up to the CEO and ask: "Which persona are you?" If they don't have an answer, explain, "We are designing *only* for these target customers and if you're not one of them, we're not designing for you, even if you *are* the CEO!"

We also use personas when we look for UX testing participants. Rather than grabbing random people, we look for people who match these sweet spots of target customers.

If you haven't done UX research and if you don't have personas, don't just say, "We know our users." This is where confidence could accidentally slide into arrogance. Chances are there's plenty you don't know. User research is a core part of UX and shouldn't be skipped or reduced for any reason, especially not because of arrogance.

Personas are ever-present and pop up a lot. A good set of personas should be able to last a company some years, but must be redone when technology changes, user behaviors change, or the target audience shifts.

Task Set 3 – Content Analysis and Strategy

Content is your copy (wording) and media (images, videos, other multimedia). Content is definitely *not* an afterthought. It's an important part of the UX process and the user's experience. Not sure? See how you feel about a website next time they present oceans and oceans of text that you don't want to read. That's when you know they either didn't care about content strategy or did it badly.

Still not convinced? Ask me about the client whose website proudly claimed that they sell to: "All 52 USA states." What impression do you have of a company with typos, poor grammar, or an inability to count 50 American states? What impression do you have of a company who outsourced copy for an American audience to a country that doesn't know how many states are in the USA?

Your content must reflect how users think about the topic or information on the screen. You can't write noticeably above or below their reading ability or level of knowledge. It's a fine balance and that's why we bring in expert UX writers and content strategists.

People have very little attention span. Nearly zero. (I can't believe you're still reading *this*! I'm honored!) Expert UX copywriters must write for attention span as well. Don't put ten paragraphs on the page when the UX team knows people are willing to read possibly two sentences.

A guy from a Fortune 50 company told me that his teams have only been working with UX specialists for around three years; it's still new to them. But one of the main places his company is seeing noticeable ROI is in content strategy.

Their expert content strategist does user testing on variations of how they describe their products and services. That way, before the site or page goes live, they are confident that the information is easy to understand and really resonates with their target customers.

The next example is possibly the opposite of that.

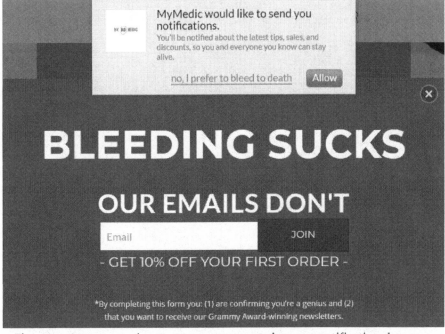

Figure 12: A pop-up trying to get you to agree to browser notifications has a "no" option where you express that you prefer death to notifications. And it has a second pop-up (double-bad UX) trying to get you to join their mailing list.

Content is important. Brand voice is important. Microcopy—brief instances of copy in strategic places—is important. Having to click on, "I prefer to bleed to death," because you don't want to join an email mailing list, considered a form of bullying by some UX professionals. I found the above example in my LinkedIn feed with the hashtag #confirmshaming, which is a thing!

Perhaps someone in marketing thought this pop-up would go viral, forgetting that things can go viral for negative reasons and create negative buzz. All of the comments under this screen shot on LinkedIn were negative. I'm now aware of this company but I'm not impressed by a medical and survival kits company making lighthearted references to bleeding or dying.

But they have obviously decided to go all-in on this content approach. The description of their tourniquet reads: "Tired of bleeding to death? Us too. Thanks to the R.A.T.S. Tourniquet team and the bearded giants at ReadyMan, we can stop doing just that. How, you ask? Here is your first-class ticket to living: RATS [sic] Tourniquet."

Did this copy test well with the target audience, people visiting this site for medical and survival kits? Did their research show that those people are whimsical and comical about death and catastrophic experiences? If proper UX research and testing show that this copy is a winner, then that wins over any opinion I have.

But if people are buying here *in spite of the copy* and not because of it—which I suspect—then the company shouldn't tell itself the content really works. It's always best to do research and testing to make sure that your brand voice and copy really speak to your customer, no pun intended.

Task Set 4 – Information Architecture (IA)

Information Architecture has to do with hierarchies, structure, and taxonomies. This could be site navigation or how products are categorized in an eCommerce database. We want to make sure customers will easily find products by categories, metadata, and filters.

What's for lunch? There's a well-known restaurant review website that offers this list of additional categories when you have searched for restaurants:

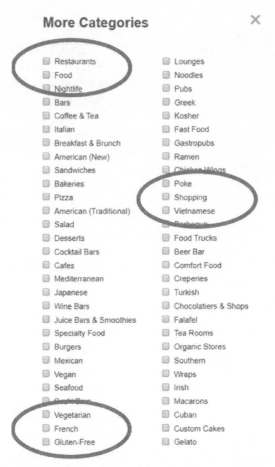

Figure 13: Poor Information Architecture on a restaurant search site.

We can quickly notice a few things about it.

1. It's not in any particular order, not even alphabetical. If you want to find gluten-free or vegetarian options, you will have to skim each one until you find that checkbox. This means a lot of thinking and work for customers, who at the very least would expect a list in alphabetical order or some other order we've researched and found to be meaningful to users.

2. There are also things in this list that make no sense. You searched for restaurants. Why is "Restaurants" a possible sub-category of restaurants? Why is "Food" a possible sub-category when all restaurants serve food? Why is "Shopping" on this list, and what does it even mean in this context? Elements have to be *meaningful to customers*, which requires empathy and a great ability to create taxonomies.

3. It's flat, meaning there are no sub-categories with organized items. For example, you could have Bars and then have sub-categories of Beer Bars, Wine Bars, even Juice Bars, but also Pubs, Lounges, Cocktail Bars, etc.

Organization is what IA is all about and this ocean of checkboxes appears to have been thrown together randomly with no thought put into how to make this easier or more logical for customers.

Lacking inside information on the company that built this, these might be categories that restaurants added themselves on the fly and the company hasn't paid any attention to them. At the very least, someone with an IA specialty should have a look at this and reorganize it. Won't someone *please* think of the customers' brains?!

Task Set 5 – Interaction Design (IxD)

Interaction Design is what most people think of when they imagine UX. These are our wireframes and prototypes, the blueprints of our designs. These would show process flows, layouts, menus, interactions, paths, choices, and so much more.

Figure 14: A medium-fidelity wireframe.

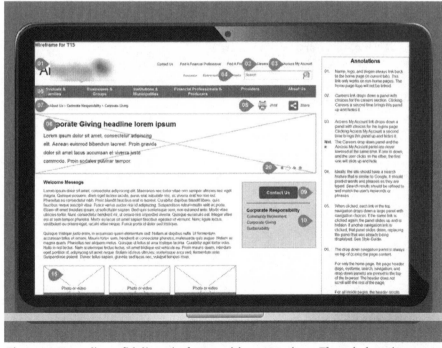

Figure 15: A medium-fidelity wireframe with annotations. These help point out ideas or interactions that people wouldn't know by looking at a static wireframe.

UX prototypes are like wireframes brought to life. They are clickable, interactive digital mock-ups. We don't have to write code to make a prototype. We have software that helps us create these quickly. If you are just looking to click through something and show a path, many companies use Invision [invisionapp.com]. But my favorite is Axure [axure.com] because you can make the prototype very realistic. It has conditional logic, variables, mobile swiping gestures, dragging and dropping, and all kinds of event triggers. You can prototype for just about any type of device.

I suggest that UX practitioners move increasingly into realistic prototyping for the complex pages and flows that our software now has. It's no longer "this page links to this page." There is so much that can happen on one screen. There might be variations by whether someone is a customer or not, what level they are paying for, and where we need to show error messages or states. Click-through models are not enough to communicate what UX designers are creating; we should be moving towards more realistic rapid prototyping without taxing dev teams to write code.

Why do UX prototyping? You can:

- Brainstorm
- Collaborate
- Iterate
- Explore solutions
- Pitch to investors
- Test the prototype to see if the solution connects well with the target audience(s)
- Deliver an interactive model to developers or other teammates, which is often preferred over pages of documentation.

Task Set 6 – User Testing

Now the interaction designs get user testing (you might also hear "usability testing") which happens during the UX process and before Engineering writes a line of code. We need to make sure that the idea and the execution are fantastic for our target customers. We don't want Engineering to build it until we're sure this is what will be built.

User testing will bring to light any flaws, giving UX the chance to iterate on ideas, which sends us back to interaction design work.

There are five reasons a feature or concept should be tested during the UX process, well before developers have built it or released anything, even a beta or MVP, to the public:

1. **Best uses of Engineering's time and resources.** If you want testing participants to see a finished product created by engineers, you have to build that product and then test it for bugs. If UX testing brings needed changes to light, developers have to re-build and QA has to re-test. If UX testing showed a larger failure of the concept, this might mean that Engineering's time was completely wasted as this is not code that will end up anywhere. The concept would have to be rethought, redesigned, and freshly tested.

    We want UX to get fast feedback, iterate, and be agile. Waiting for Engineering to build or rebuild our prototypes or real versions slows UX down, which will have a negative domino effect.

2. **Iterate behind the scenes.** When companies just build it and just ship it, then iterate on it and build and ship again, this means that customers are seeing a variety of versions. They are seeing the work in progress and watching the sausage being made. This is often a frustrating and confusing experience, requiring customers to keep re-learning a system that's evolving. It's better to iterate behind the scenes in the UX process and to be clear with testers that it's a prototype or demonstration version.

3. **Monitoring and measuring.** If a new concept is released live, UX researchers don't have a good way to monitor how it's going. With user testing, they can watch people use it, ask them questions, and get the type of feedback UX needs to determine if something is ready or needs another iteration. UX always wants to know the why—the qualitative— and not just the what or how many. How are users spending, converting, engaging, etc? Avoiding proper UX testing makes it harder to diagnose and fix issues or customer pain points because we often get quantitative data without the qualitative.

4. **UX testing pays for itself.** UX testing is not a huge expense. Some third-party testing tools want under $100 per testing participant; some require a minimum annual commitment of a few thousand dollars. Either way, these are not huge expenses given the company's overall budget for the software development process and the importance of early testing feedback.

For the first round of testing, the rule of thumb is to use five people. It's a small sample, but it's also a quick way to find the most obvious flaws early. For future rounds, you can 5 to 15 people, especially when testing would benefit from more participants representing more personas.

Rounds of user testing nearly always cost less and move faster than making programmers build something they might have to undo or build again.

5. **User testing resolves arguments.** If your company doesn't allow UX specialists to make the final decision on how a product is designed, then you might find UX in conflict with Product, Engineering, or a key stakeholder when there are varying ideas of what should be built and released to the customer. Or what if UX has two strong ideas and they are wondering which connects better with customers? The solution here is user testing.

UX can prototype the concepts. It's best to boil the competition down to the best two designs, especially if you can already find compromises across ideas and team members. This means we're not testing what UX wants versus. what Product likes versus. what the engineering head likes versus. what the scrum master thinks sounds like a good idea versus. what the CEO's life partner likes.

User testing lets the customers speak for themselves, have their voices heard, and helps you find the right direction for the features or product. It resolves arguments by providing teams with hard quantitative and qualitative data that tells everybody which idea is likely to bring the most customer satisfaction.

Some companies use an experimentation model in which the final concept is released to a certain percentage of current customers or users, metrics are watched, and then they decide if they will remove the feature or scale the experiment to more users. But dropping an update on real and possibly paying customers shouldn't be the first time we get feedback. It's too risky.

Whether or not you are experimenting with releases, user testing will give you confidence that the product you are deploying is a match to users' real needs, habits, and motivations. It was researched with them, designed for them, and tested with them. It's not User-Centered Design if you don't include users at every step of the process.

User testing proves that proposed designs, workflows, and screens will lead to the best outcomes and customer experiences.

Figure 16: Great Monty Python moment. A building architect shows a model of proposed apartments he claims are sturdy and fireproof. While presenting, his model catches on fire and collapses.

In 1970, *Monty Python's Flying Circus* featured a sketch about an architect. The architect is showing his apartment building model to his potential client, two businessmen. While the architect is describing how structurally sound the building is thanks to the use of steel and concrete, the model starts collapsing. When he mentions how by not using any wood, they've nearly completely removed the risk of fire, the model bursts into flames. The embarrassed architect tells the businessmen perhaps the central structure needs more strengthening.

The businessmen ask if it will make the building cost more and the architect says that it will. The businessmen decide they don't want to spend the money on that; they'll just aim for tenants who weigh less and don't move around so much, and they'll hope for good weather.

The businessmen are fine with releasing this heavily-flawed concept to the paying public, and they don't want to spend more time or money to make the building better or safer. **Does this scenario hit close to home?** That's exactly like companies not wanting to budget for UX experts to do real UX work. *We'll just release this and hope we don't end up a customer, PR, or stock price disaster.*

This is precisely why UX prototypes and tests. If our UX model crashes and burns in small or large ways, the good news is that Engineering hasn't spent any time on it yet. UX can fix the problems, iterate, and test again. This is the *fast feedback and iteration* everybody wants.

Task Set 7: Iteration and Refinement

Testing rarely shows 100% perfection. We often find small or large flaws in the design, steps, layouts, or other UX elements.

Allow time and budget for UX to learn from their testing and iterate on the designs. After each refinement, UX typically wants to test again. That's a good thing. You don't like to release code until you feel confident that it's bug-free; UX doesn't want to declare a design finalized until it tests well with real or archetypal users.

Task Set 8: Visual Design

Visual design is considered part of UX, but that doesn't mean UX practitioners are all artists. Just like we're not all copywriters. We're not all expert researchers. UX has many sub-specialties that are often separate jobs. Visual design affects the user experience so it's considered part of the User-Centered Design process.

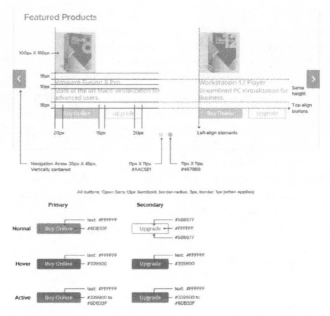

Figure 17: Sample from VMWare's public UI pattern library.

This figure is from VMWare's public site for their UI pattern library. Once a visual designer has done the graphic design, typography, iconography, photo selection, and other things they specialize in, they typically deliver comps and specs.

The comps show the interface fully designed, sometimes with final approved copy. And then they spec everything out with measurements, spacing, sizing, and other numbers so developers know exactly where everything goes. This is clearer and more standardized than developers guessing how much space goes where or what color something is.

Visual designers might instead or additionally deliver a component, pattern, style, or UI library. This allows UX and developers to work from pre-designed, standardized elements.

A visual designer will deliver the blueprint Engineering needs to follow, but if you're reading this book, you've probably seen visual design specs and style guides before!

Task Set 7: Documentation

While documentation could be seen as a separate step, it's more likely that as UX goes through the UCD process, various documents are being delivered. These might include competitive research reports, a heuristic analysis, sitemap, process flows, annotated wireframes, prototypes, and anything else that'll help Engineering build, test, and see their process through. This book won't explain all of these, but this list is a moment for you to realize how many deliverables UX could have throughout the full UCD process.

To wrap up our look at User-Centered Design, the process is, "Discover, design, build, test, monitor, and iterate." Hey, that sounds familiar... is this UX or software development?

Both. There are great parallels between our processes. We are allies!

DIFFERENCES BETWEEN UX AND UI

UX and UI are often confused. One way to learn to tell them apart is to hit the websites of some well-known universities to check what types of classes you must take to get a degree in UX or a degree in visual design.

UX practitioners are concerned with functions, processes, organization, layouts, and usability, so they study:

- Cognitive psychology
- Theories of human-centered design
- Qualitative research methods
- Data visualization
- Interaction design & prototyping
- Usability studies

A visual (UI) designer is normally focused more on the aesthetics of these elements, including color choices, typography, spacing, and branding. They study:

- Typography
- Digital photography
- Branding principles
- Motion graphics
- Semiotics (the study of signs and symbols)
- Color fundamentals

Think of your UX specialist as a building's architect, and your UI specialist as your interior designer. You need both; they do important, but very different jobs.

"UX versus. UI" is a cousin of "function versus form." UX is the function, focused on layouts, processes, interactivity, features, steps, and choices. It's about psychology and natural human behavior.

UI, the form, is more about brand, mood, and feel. It absolutely affects UX and usability, which is why these people should be collaborators. If you peek back at the User-Centered Design model, you will see that visual design is considered part of user experience. Companies doing it right will have visual designers managed by UX leaders.

The visual design is sometimes the last piece of the UX puzzle. If you are getting fully designed UX deliverables, you probably hired an artist, who may or may not be the right person for a job (see the lack of overlap above). It also means that every time you change the UX, someone must redo pixel-perfect visual design, typography, branding, etc.

If the layouts and interactions aren't great or the wireframes or prototypes don't test well, who cares if it's pretty or if it matches our brand? It's more than OK to do "medium-fidelity" UX work, which is more grayscale and placeholder than completely designed comps, which are often called "full-fidelity" or "high-fidelity."

You can absolutely run user testing with medium-fidelity wireframes and prototypes. I'm not an artist; I'm a UX specialist. All of my artistic talent ended up in music, which means I mostly work and test in medium fidelity.

THE FOUR HORSEMEN OF BAD UX®

"The Four Horsemen of Bad UX" is my creation aimed at helping UX and non-UX workers recognize how and why the interface we already have or the one we're designing is likely to be a poor choice for our target customers. The Four Horsemen might be summoned based on feedback we get in user testing, or they might be problems we can notice ourselves.

Remember that you should put yourself in the shoes of one or more personas when checking for The Four Horsemen.

The Four Horsemen of Bad UX, along with some examples of what users might be thinking, are:

- **Frustration**—Broken expectations make people flustered, angry.
  - o "I wanted to apply for the job, but they wanted me to fill out a huge form with 10 essay questions. And I'm on my phone!"

- o "I wanted to create an account, but they kept rejecting my password for not fitting into their password rules."
- o "I'm trying to change my phone number, but this site keeps popping up a mobile alphabet keyboard instead of a number pad."
- o "This site says it only works with Internet Explorer. What year is this?!"
- **Confusion**—Broken expectations make people feel confused, unsure, lost.
  - o "I wanted to check on the status of my claim, but couldn't find my claims after logging in."
  - o "I thought this link was going to take me where I wanted to go, but instead, they tried to sell me some other product."
  - o "Search results seemed disorganized. It was hard to find what I really wanted."
  - o "I just want to pay my bill. Where can I do that on this site?"
- **Disappointment**—Broken expectations make people disheartened, disappointed, and like they wasted their time.
  - o "I thought I was going to be able to change my address online, but it turns out I have to call the company."
  - o "I filtered my search results to only items available in my size, but the item detail page said this actually wasn't available in my size."
  - o "The site told me I could buy tickets by where I wanted to sit but that feature looked disabled."
  - o "I took their little quiz but the website said it didn't have enough information to estimate how much I'd need to retire. What a waste of my time!"
- **Distraction**—The most eye-catching element is not (that) important to the user.
  - o Elements that are nearly impossible to *not* look at, yet they are not the CTA (Call to Action, like the main button).
  - o "Cool things," intro movies, background movies, and social media are in the way.
  - o Looping animations (that won't stop) like carousels and marketing messages.
  - o Auto-playing audio or video, especially when the user can't figure out how to stop it.
  - o Busy side columns. Any side columns! We don't read newspaper-style anymore. We're used to reading one thing linearly.
  - o eCommerce pages where there is a lot going on before you get to the "Add to Cart" button, the #1 element we hope people interact with.

One easy—though potentially "not safe for work"—way to remember all Four Horsemen is this mnemonic: *If you don't remove bad UX from your interface, your project will be **FCDD***. (Read FCDD as a word out loud a few times but not at work or when children are around.) Now you won't be able to forget FCDD: frustrated, confused, disappointed, and distracted.

You're   welcome.

THREE INGREDIENTS FOR SUCCESS

People, Process, Culture, and Values
(OK that's four, but stick with me...)

There are three ingredients for UX integration success:

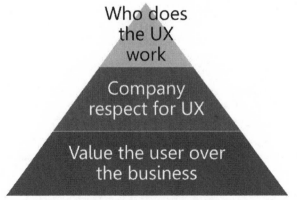

Figure 18: Three Ingredients for Success

At the foundation is **valuing the user over the business**. These are your corporate values, your promise to the customer, the rally cry that unifies your workers. You must decide the user's needs, motivations, habits, and even safety are more important than what the business stakeholders might want or what could make a quick buck.

If you need your dentist to fill some small cavities, he doesn't instead suggest that he remove the teeth and replace them with implants because it makes him more money. You hate the mechanic that wants to do more work on your car than the car really needs. When you know a company is doing that to you, you hate them. So why do this with your product?

Focus on the user, and trust that the revenue will be there if you build the right thing for the right people. It's about putting stories and features into roadmaps that will solve customer pain points or innovate on something they need. It's about adjusting business processes to start building better products.

Horror Story: Valuing the Business (and Potential Profit) Over the User

The best example we have of a company that puts the business before the user - as of April 2019 when I'm writing this - is Facebook.

In every product it releases or acquires (Facebook, Facebook Messenger, Instagram, etc.), Facebook doesn't care about users' preferences, privacy, needs, or pain points. Facebook has filed a patent to listen to you in your home so they can tell advertisers if you watch their TV commercials or do other things while they're are on.

Multiple people have reported that after having a live conversation with someone, Facebook served them ads relating to the conversation they just had. Tech blogs like to claim that people "just don't understand retargeting and lookalike audiences," but most of the reports I've read came from techies who found it beyond coincidental that they just said a restaurant name out loud and nearly immediately got an ad for it.

I've seen ads for a product immediately after mentioning something related to that product's industry to my boyfriend. Harmless? My conversation with my boyfriend was in WhatsApp, which is supposed to be encrypted end-to-end.

Instagram won't show me the image I'm trying to share to a Story as I create the Story. Why not? I blocked Instagram's access to my phone's microphone. I get a blank screen and a message reminding me to give access to the camera... but I did give access to the camera. This is clearly a "dark pattern" (we'll talk more about those later) because Instagram wants to bully you into giving microphone access. If this were a bug, QA should have found it by now. I've been experiencing this problem through multiple releases over many months.

Facebook makes changes to the way their product looks and works to manipulate you, even to make things work opposite of what would be natural, intuitive, and helpful. Many people are now aware of the "experiments" Facebook has admitted to where they wanted to see if they could make people more depressed. Don't worry, Facebook, you've truly created a system that inspires depression and negativity. You're tops!

These decisions all put the business before the user. There is no way that UX workers at Facebook are truly empowered to build what customers need over what the business stakeholders want; I'd like to imagine that there is no UX team in the United States that would want to manipulate any country's elections in any direction. I would hope there is no UX team on the planet that designs a system that deliberately shows you more depressing posts more often to see if they can mess with your emotions. And I can't imagine a UX team that decided that every time something goes well for liberals in the USA in 2018-2019, we should show liberal users of Instagram right-wing propaganda in the "Explore" area of Instagram (which is my personal experience).

We now know stories of people who were shunned by friends and family or ended up in real danger because their conservative communities found out they were LGBT. And how did people find out what was supposed to be a secret? Facebook told their friends that they had joined a Facebook Group related to LGBT issues. As of early 2018, just before I deleted my Facebook account, it was still doing that. Facebook wanted me to join all kinds of Facebook groups because Friend X or Friend Y was in those groups.

A business wins when its customers win. Facebook appeared to be winning, but as their truths unfold, Facebook is losing more and more. People are too lazy to switch and there are no viable alternatives. When a one does exist, I believe Facebook will go the way of MySpace, but with a dishonorable place in history.

Facebook isn't the only example of a company putting business goals ahead of user needs, but they are a strong one with which everybody is familiar.

The middle of the pyramid reminds you to make sure that the **culture at your company respects UX**. This involves process *and* behavior. Your company must rise above the all-too-common misunderstanding of and disrespect for UX, and improve workflows, staffing, and culture. Processes must include UX specialists from the earliest conversations and planning through product design, engineering, release, and post-release monitoring.

At the top of the pyramid, we ask to whom your company gives UX work. **Have you hired qualified and experienced UX specialists**? Whether they are internal to the company, freelancers, or from an outside agency, it's important to choose wisely. Going cheap by having people who aren't trained or experienced UX practitioners just push out wireframes or run flawed research won't help you in the short or long term. Hire carefully.

These three work together in that hiring the wrong UX people will give your company ammunition to disrespect or circumvent UX. Not valuing the user over anything else means that wrong decisions will be made in all areas at all levels. And not showing respect for the great UX experts you hired, not giving them the time they need, and not following their designs, topples the pyramid.

Perhaps nobody can help a company for whom the bottom of the pyramid is broken. DevOps ICU doesn't attempt to change this type of company. I suggest that talented workers who want to make a real difference polish up that resume and LinkedIn, and just move on.

Most of the book covers the middle of the pyramid. This chapter dives into the top, answering many common questions about who should do UX work.

Hiring the right people to do UX work is so important yet so often done incorrectly. Let's take a closer look at some of the common mistakes and suggested approaches in the hiring process.

CAN YOU COMBINE A UX JOB WITH A UI JOB? CAN UI EXPERTS DO UX JOBS?

You'll often see jobs for a UX/UI Designer. Sometimes they will call it a Product Designer and expect both UX expertise *and* fantastic visual design skills. Sometimes a Product Designer job is purely UX. UX job titles are still confusing to those inside and outside of the practice so we rely more on the job description and required skills than what the job was called.

Like we learned that UX and UI talents, skills, and education don't overlap, UX and UI jobs don't naturally overlap. Someone great at designing form could be awful at designing function, and vice-versa. Being talented in UX doesn't mean you're a great artist. Being a great artist doesn't mean you are a great UX designer. Many people are sure they are great at both, but it's rarer than people want to admit.

An example of hiring going wrong is a job listing from 2018 for a Senior UX Designer at a Fortune 100 company. The company wanted at least six years of experience across the full User-Centered Design process including UX research, design, and testing—one person who could do it all. They also wanted UX prototyping, which is a UX sub-specialty that not every practitioner has. But at least all of these requirements fell into the general UX skill set.

The company also asked for "high-fidelity" prototyping, which as we discussed earlier means fully visually designed and therefore requiring a great artist.

But swallow your coffee because the job listing also said that 20% of the worker's time would be doing illustrations, possibly for the marketing team. That means this person must be a professional illustrator, someone who can draw. Not every UX practitioner is an amazing visual designer. Not every visual designer is an amazing illustrator.

The recruiter told me that this worker would lead a UX team tasked with fixing the company's shameful and low-rated smartphone app. This app is so bad even employees are leaving one-star ratings complaining about how hard it is for them to use and how hard their job is when customers direct app anger at them.

Side note: I'm not impressed by a company trying to hire a UX team leader or manager but paying less by giving the job a senior-level title.

This job listing highlights the hiring manager's bizarre idea that this worker will have *spare time* to take on illustration. It also shines a light on a Fortune 100 that desperately needs a deeply-experienced, T-shaped Senior UX Designer with app and retail experience. "T-shaped" implies that someone has depth in one area, represented by the long, vertical bar of the T, but also has other related skills (though perhaps not as deep a specialty), represented by the horizontal bar of the T.

This job will likely be given to a visual designer and illustrator. This job has a UX title but with these requirements, jobs like this one are often filled by excellent artists whose artwork would impress us all but who typically have little UX experience or understanding of the User-Centered Design process. We'll look later in this chapter at why this can end up a disaster.

This job description may not sound strange or unfamiliar to you because many companies do this, believing they can save money hiring one person to do two very different jobs. They see "Designer" in a UX title and "Designer" in an artist title and assume there is a huge overlap between the two. If you've been reading this book, you've already learned that a UX degree and a UI degree often have zero overlap (or close to it).

Would your company hire a software developer with little experience or formalized process? Workers with "Engineer" somewhere in their title aren't interchangeable. People great at one engineering job may be terrible at another.

When you prioritize hiring someone with artistic talents for a UX job, you are often giving the job to the wrong person.

How about people claiming to be Jacks-of-All-Trades? I once interviewed a guy for a UX job. He said he was great at UX, visual design, and front-end development. What are the odds! I asked him what his approach is to UX projects, which meant I was listening for him to talk about the User-Centered Design process. His answer was, "Yeah, I just open Photoshop or Illustrator and I design right into that."

If you interviewed a programmer and she showed you finished code, you might ask, "How did you approach this project? What was your process?" If she said she opened up her environment and wrote some code, the red flags would be flying in the gale force winds.

When we take UX out of the story, of course it sounds ridiculous. But when you aren't that familiar with UX and you are trying to hire for UX, it can be easy to miss these things. You don't know the right answer, so most answers sound good.

THE "AMERICAN IDOL AUDITIONEE" EFFECT (DUNNING-KRUGER)

Why aren't candidates more honest about how good they really are at UX? Why do so many artists assume they can "do UX" because they "design interfaces" or "make wireframes?" Are these people lying to you? Not necessarily. While UX impostors are a problem out in the real world, in many cases it's simply an issue of self-awareness.

Many of us have seen American Idol auditions where the singer is – let's face it - terrible. Not talented. Definitely not going to make it to the next round. When these people are rejected immediately, they are heartbroken. Crying. Angry. Resentful. They are sure the judges got it wrong. "Wait, let me try another song."

What went wrong? These people might be very passionate about singing. They might have taken lessons and practice often. They might sing at church or at karaoke. They might have lots of friends and family telling them they are great. And now they are surprised that nobody everybody finds them to be amazing.

It's the Dunning-Kruger effect. People with poor abilities or no natural talent combined with poor self-awareness aren't able to accurately assess their own level of talent or ability. We see this all the time but "bad" American Idol auditions are a great, concrete example of Dunning-Kruger in action.

Remember that to an expert, a non-expert, even one claiming to be an expert, is quickly found out. I illustrate this with an old joke where a rich man buys a boat, a captain's outfit, a captain's hat, and proudly announces to his parents that he's a captain! His father finally tells him that to Mama and Papa, he's a captain. To him, he's a captain. But to a captain, he's no captain!

I'm a bad artist. If I ever tried to apply for hybrid UX/UI jobs that required great visual design skills, I'd be found out immediately. A real artist/captain will look at my work and know that I'm no artist/captain. The same is true for artists, programmers, and others who claim to do UX work without good process or natural talent. Show their work to me or another high-level, veteran UX expert and we're going to know if we have a UX practitioner, an impostor, or a well-intentioned person with low self-awareness.

UNHAPPY WITH UX? YOU PROBABLY HIRED THE WRONG PEOPLE

A very talented developer emailed me asking if I do 1:1 sessions. Yes, I do private training and mentoring! He had a job interview in about 10 days for a UX Engineer job. Hmmm, I asked him what he was hoping I'd teach or explain in the next week.

He imaged that during the interview, they might ask him to "design a UI" or a product. He would need to gather information like user needs, user goals, assumptions, and constraints. He expected the interview might require him to draw a user flow and possibly whiteboard the app or product, indicating technical constraints.

Wow, that's quite an interview! And what UX background did he have? None. He was a developer who had never done any UX. His LinkedIn looked very impressive and I'm sure any company would benefit from hiring him as a developer... but how did a guy with zero UX on his resume apply for—not to mention get an interview scheduled for—a UX job? Why does he now think he can learn all the right UX things to say in an interview happening in 10 days?

When companies don't understand UX, they don't know what to look for. They might hire someone like this developer because he looks like a great developer and hey, UX is so easy anybody can do it, no experience or education required.

These are mistakes that companies must stop making. He's a fantastic engineer but could he be a fantastic UX engineer? Not necessarily and not while he has zero UX knowledge or education.

When I speak at events, non-UX roles want me to advise or comment on their UX horror stories.

- **Poor collaboration.** UX spent months building something and when Engineering saw it, they realized it couldn't be built. Good UX people would know to collaborate early with Engineering without being prompted, but these UX workers never did that and nobody seemed to be managing them and pushing them to collaborate with Engineering.
- **Hiring workers with little UX knowledge or experience.** Companies that didn't really understand UX hired someone who said they were into UX

and understood the UX process... but had no UX experience or education on their resume. Heads up, liking UX and knowing a few things about the process qualifies you as much as liking Ruby and knowing a little about how to generally approach coding would qualify me.

- **UX workers are "artsy."** I hear complaints about UX workers who are really artsy, very into the appearance of things, but produce designs that teammates feel won't work well for the customer. These UX workers magically also tend to believe they don't need to do user testing. These people don't sound like real UX specialists. Again, it's easy to hire an artist to do UX work when your company doesn't really understand UX and doesn't know how to interpret a portfolio of work or what interview questions to ask.
- **Short order cooks.** I've heard about UX workers who were non-creative and didn't solve problems. They only wireframed exactly what you asked for and nothing more. This left product managers and other roles feeling like they had to do the UX work, even wireframing what they want UX to wireframe, which *really* makes no sense. These UX workers are probably "short order cooks" and not "interface scientists," which I'll explain next.

You can see why I'm sometimes brought in to help companies hire and build teams. It's hard to hire for a job you don't understand. If you asked me to assess and select the best back-end developer from a pile of candidates, I wouldn't get it right. I have no idea what to look for. This is what happens in many companies when it comes to UX. We must change how we hire UX specialists.

DO YOU NEED A SHORT ORDER COOK OR AN INTERFACE SCIENTIST?

UX practitioners, visual designers, graphic designers, artists, and other creative people can be roughly split into two general buckets: people who do their best work when you tell them exactly what you need, and people who do their best work when you present them with the problem to be solved. I call these "short order cooks" and "interface scientists."

You want two scrambled eggs with bacon, you get exactly two eggs and bacon, and you'll be surprised and disappointed if you get anything else or some creative variation. Short order cooks (SOCs) design the exact idea someone can concretely express. Their main focus is to get the task done quickly and accurately. A great SOC is excellent at understanding instructions so that they can prepare the correct assets, files, and designs. They might be creative but are most often delivering on someone else's vision or instructions.

The SOC will normally follow a request down to the last detail, even if the request isn't a great idea or might work against the usability. It's often more important to them to do what they've been asked versus getting creative, offering other ideas, or taking the project in a new direction.

But then there are the times when you know you want breakfast but you're not sure what to have. The answers and choices are open, you just want the best thing for you today, and you're open to whatever that is. Interface scientists would rather be given problems and questions than proposed solutions. They are typically unhappy when told to design or wireframe someone else's idea. Their strengths are more in critical thinking, problem solving, possible outcomes, and (often) cognitive psychology. Interface scientists have a process informed by research and validated by testing.

The interface scientist doesn't want to "just take orders." They want to experiment with creative ideas and possible concepts. It's more important to learn, design, test, and iterate, even if that approach opens cans of worms or suggests that the project needs to go in another direction. They might have a pre-made set of components, but will always choose the best solution over what they happened to have handy or pre-made.

Visual, graphic, and UX designers can fall into either bucket. You have met highly creative visual designers who were interface scientists. You have met less creative UX designers who were happier and "did a better job" when they could just wireframe the idea the product manager described.

You get very different work from these two types of people. Workplaces get it wrong when they put the wrong type in place.

UX practitioners should be interface scientists. If your UX designer is just wireframing what the CEO likes today, that's not really UX work. That's being a pair of hands (and a short order cook) that turns the CEO's ideas, declarations, or whiteboards into what looks like UX documentation. A UX practitioner using the User-Centered Design process is informed by research and validates or invalidates hypotheses and designs through user testing.

It's not UX without incorporating the users and their needs into a valuable product. If you're not allowing a UX designer to work through the User-Centered Design process or you're giving them orders of how this feature will lay out or work, then you want a short order cook.

"I'm not getting what I need from my UX designer," a product manager at a Fortune 100 company told me. "I can't seem to get what I want from him unless I wireframe it and tell him exactly what to do." This product manager wants an interface scientist, but his company hired a short order cook.

"They said they hired me for my extensive experience in this industry, my seniority, and my subject matter expertise. But the UX lead just wanted me to wireframe her ideas," lamented a principal UX architect, who soon quit that job. The lead wanted a short order cook but the company hired an interface scientist.

When hiring, companies must consider talent, skill, experience, abilities, process, approach, and other factors. But for better matches, they must also look at whether the candidate shines as a short order cook or as an interface scientist.

WHY SHOULDN'T A PRODUCT MANAGER WIREFRAME THEIR IDEA?

A product manager told me that expressing ideas in user stories and words doesn't seem like enough. He could make a wireframe to describe the idea and possibly gain consensus around ideas that could meet customer ideas. What could be wrong with that?

Product managers who show me their wireframes are often somewhat or completely sold on their own ideas, especially if they have already "gained consensus" on it. It's often, "Design it this way," or, "This is my idea, start with this," versus, "This is just me sketching what I couldn't put into words."

OK, but the product manager's job is to put these visions into stories (made of words), and also to ensure product-market fit, check for customer value, viability, feasibility, and measure product success. UX is your partner on many of those! But back to our product manager...

What kind of information can you *not* put in user stories? The feature, vision, story, pain point, or problem plus related data are what product managers are supposed to communicate to UX (plus that documentation is there for deversus, QA, and other interested parties).

UX uses all of our steps, tasks, research, testing, and more to *solve* the problem that the product manager describes. But nearly 100% of product managers who give me a wireframe have started with solution-based thinking. There are many companies in which the product manager doesn't want UX to think about the problem. They want them to start with the potential solution the product manager has chosen. Then you want a short order cook in a world where the best UX practitioners are interface scientists.

This also denies UX most of its reason for being: the research, design, iteration, and testing behind solutions. Product managers don't do the research UX does. And many product managers don't have the talent, skills, or education UX specialists have.

Wireframing and product design are rarely in the product manager job listing (and shouldn't be part of the job), so if you are spending time on that, you might not be focused on the right things. You will get more out of talented UX practitioners by bringing them problems, not prescribing them solutions.

On behalf of UX, we invite product managers, business analysts, and other non-UX roles to stop wireframing. Tell UX the problems, and they will solve them.

WHY SHOULDN'T ENGINEERING AND/OR PRODUCT MANAGERS DESIGN THE PRODUCT?

This book should really called, "Everybody Stop Wireframing—You Don't Work in UX."

A product manager asked me why many UX practitioners feel that non-UX roles are "bad" at UX and shouldn't be designing products. There are three key reasons:

1. **UX is way more than wireframing.** Non-UX roles who have decided to "do UX" on a project often just make wireframes. UX's Interaction Design work is based on process, research, data, experience, education, the "laws of UX," and cognitive psychology. Which of those are non-UX roles using? Often none. They tend to believe that wireframing is sketching screen layouts, it looks easy, and anybody can do that. But you know now that it's so much more than that.

2. **UX requires mountains of empathy.** Empathy isn't as common as we believe. Caring for others, showing compassion, and being kind still aren't necessarily displays of empathy. Empathy is truly putting yourself into someone else's existence and seeing their world through their eyes. That means whatever they believe, whatever they think, and whatever they're likely to do are a role you have to assume, even if you

disagree with their beliefs, don't like how they think, and think what they do is stupid.

UX practitioners must method act themselves into being our personas. But many people can't get out of their own heads, especially when trying to design interfaces. They automatically design *what they would want, what they would like,* or *what they think looks nice.*

At a DevOps ICU interactive workshop in late 2018, one of the exercises was the task of creating a customer journey map as Kristi, a young housewife, who is researching insurance she and her husband might choose to buy. The engineers struggled with this exercise and even admitted (out loud) that it was very hard to not imagine themselves, how *they* would search for insurance, and how *they* would make decisions.

Empathy doesn't come naturally to everybody, and that's OK.

3. **Non-UX practitioners often do flawed or skewed "UX research."** Lean books tell you to get "out of the building" and "away from the mirror." They are hoping you won't lock yourself into a trendy co-working space and just build *what you like.*

   Sadly, many people trying to do their own Lean UX research ask wrong or naturally-biased questions. "Do you like this?" "Would you use this?" "Would your friends use this?" These sound like good research questions but are never asked in UX research because people like to sound positive even if they *don't* like your proposed product or concept and wouldn't use it. People want to say, "Yes, I'd use this and pay for it," even if they dislike it or believe it should be free. They're just being polite. File it with, "Do I look fat in this?" Of course not!

To sum up, without a UX process, solid and unbiased UX research, and very high empathy allowing you to really imagine processes and experiences through the eyes of another, you're probably not good at UX. It's OK! We're all good at something! You might not be naturally talented at UX tasks. I'm terrible at art and Social Studies. We all have our weaknesses and strengths.

These are the same reasons why artists, visual designers, and graphic designers are sometimes amazing at aesthetics but not great at UX work... and not really doing UX work, even when they say they are.

CAN WE HIRE (ONLY) JUNIORS?

There's nothing wrong with hiring juniors and entry level workers. They have to start somewhere! You may want to give them a chance.

However, I have seen companies hire one or a few juniors and nobody above them. There is no UX department or UX leadership, sometimes no experienced, senior UX practitioners. Juniors often don't work out well when they are isolated on an island. They need other more senior UX experts around them to help them refine and improve.

The same would be true for a developer fresh out of a bootcamp, a trade school, or a degree program. You wouldn't make that one junior programmer the whole software team, on an island without seniors or leaders. That's because your company values developers; we need to apply that same thinking and value to our UX workers.

Remember that even people with a recent master's degree may be a junior. Extra education is nice and can be impressive but if you are their first or second real job, they are a junior or still entry level.

Also, resist the temptation to give your UX junior a higher title than they deserve. If this is their second year doing UX, don't give them a senior title just to try to win them over as an employee. Their next hiring manager is going to expect them to be way more experienced and advanced than they may be.

Juniors can be a great addition to a company. But that's *addition* deliberately. Make sure the structure and support are there for them. If you don't have that, and especially if your company is only bringing on one or two UX employees, contractors, or freelancers, make sure those are senior with extensive experience. That way, they are self-managed and know how to handle most work, team, and office situations.

NEW TO UX? START WITH ONE SENIOR SPECIALIST

One UX practitioner is almost definitely not enough to solve all of your company's problems. But if UX is new to your company, start with one experienced senior specialist and let some of your problems be fixed. This specialist will help your DevOps begin to recover from its trip to the ICU. You can't afford to *not* hire UX experts.

Remember our pyramid from earlier in the book. If you do not highly value the user and aim to build the best product for real user needs, if your culture and processes don't support UX specialists doing their complete jobs, then hiring a great specialist still won't work for you.

Get these things right, though, and you'll quickly be sold on hiring more UX experts. But don't use inertia—"Things are probably OK the way they are now," or, "We've always done it *this* way"—as a reason to not create change. You've changed in just about every other area. You no longer send typed memos, developers aren't writing in Fortran, that Xerox copier is rarely used, and you might even be designing for smartphones.

You can't keep up, modernize, or innovate without change.

If your child said that cleaning her room seemed too hard so she wasn't even going to start to clean any of it, you probably wouldn't let her get away with such an attitude. Don't let your company act that way, either.

USER EXPERIENCE: IT'S WHAT YOU SELL

Your UX is your business. It's what you sell. And when it sucks, you're killing customer satisfaction, which affects your bottom line. The product is awful, customers are cancelling their account with you, and they can't wait to post to social media to let everybody know.

You are really gambling with your product and your reputation. Your UX practitioner or team will be designing or working on every screen of your app. Every page on your website. Your mobile responsive website. The person you choose and the team you build will be wholly or partially responsible for working with or against all of your business and DevOps goals.

Everybody has competitors. If you don't like the UX of Gmail, there are other mail systems, sites, and clients you can use. Customers are less loyal than they used to be; we can't count on someone "staying forever" if they find a competitor who has a system that is easier to use, has better features, better matches the customers' needs, or better solves real pain points.

Considering the risks, do we still want one or two juniors to be our only UX workers? Do we want Jacks-of-All-Trades (masters of none)? Do we want unicorns, purple squirrels, hybrids, or whatever they're being called this week? Do we trust our products and therefore our company to people who claim to be amazing at multiple, unrelated disciplines but in reality are often strong at one and weak at others?

You can take those risks. Or you can get smarter about who and how you hire to ensure that your UX is being worked on by experienced experts.

UX AND LEAN

"What if we found ourselves building something that nobody wanted? In that case, what did it matter if we did it on time and on budget?"
– Eric Ries

U X sometimes disagrees with product managers and engineers on how much of a product should be built and released as an MVP (Minimum Viable Product). Which is the Minimum Viable *Jogging Outfit*?

Figure 19: Which is the Minimum Viable Jogging Outfit?

Exercise: Visit https://menti.com and use code 187448. Find the question about the Minimum Viable *Jogging Outfit* and vote.

Non-UX roles believe the Minimum Viable *Jogging Outfit* is the first one since it's viable and—minus the hat—it's certainly the most minimal jogging outfit possible. UX would say the middle one, because we want something that has enough features to create customer satisfaction, traction, and adoption. Without that, the Lean universe would say you have failed.

You never get a second chance to make a first impression. This is especially true for that first time the customer installs your app or visits your website. Will this be too lean for them to really use? Enjoy? Get hooked on? Remember: you are running the risk that customers think *you're bad at this*, or, *you build broken things*.

If people were turned off by the MVP or beta, will they reinstall and give you another try for your next release? How often do you give companies second or third chances?

This is why for UX, the V in MVP stands for "valuable," not "viable." What is the leanest product we can build and release that the customer will still feel has great value? Remember that a product that is low on customer value or doesn't solve real problems for real users is likely to fail. Customers don't care if you're calling it an MVP or a beta. They'll be happy to hate it and tell everybody they know they didn't like it. People love negative attention. Or they might just uninstall, abandon, or cancel, and you've lost them.

Take it from Eric Ries—Mr. Lean himself—even if you're not doing Lean. He asked: "What if we found ourselves building something that nobody wanted? In that case, what did it matter if we did it on time and on budget?"

Go too lean and minimal, and you might be building what nobody wants. Your UX expert can help Product and Engineering prioritize stories and features to find that balance.

Horror Story: Startup Should Have Pivoted

I once did some user research for a friend's startup. My friend wanted me to start with a phone interview with her startup's biggest fan, the woman who would surely be Customer #1. I'll call her Susan.

I was asking Susan how she performs these tasks now and what her process is. After around 15 minutes of answering other questions, I asked Susan what is normally my final interview question: "If you had all the magic powers in the world and they were focused on this particular task or process, how would you make it better, faster, easier, or perfect for you?"

Susan thought for a moment. She said: "You know, I've been refining my process for nearly 20 years now. I'm happy with how I do this now." I replied: "Then you won't be [friend's] customer #1."

There was silence. "No, I guess I will not be using her system," Susan

---

sheepishly admitted. I reported this to my friend, telling her that she might not have the target audience she thinks, or that her audiences' needs are not aligned with what she plans to build. I suggested that we talk to more potential customers and see if we need to pivot or change her idea before she spends the time and money building and promoting it.

My friend didn't want me to interview anybody else and things went quiet and she carried on with her startup. A year later, she shut the startup down. When I asked why, she said nobody wanted what she was building. I knew that a year ago. I wish I could have saved her time, money, and effort. Her new (different) business is booming but it was still hard to watch a friend struggle with a troubled startup.

Sadly, many Lean, Agile, and software development books, trainings, courses, boot camps, and materials were written without UX in mind. Talking to customers and asking them leading, biased, or flawed questions does not mean you have done fantastic user research. If you are reading a book that says: "Yeah, go out and do these UX tasks, you're totally qualified!" then that book doesn't understand UX research. Of course you can ask another human questions! But my stories hopefully shine a light on the difference between that and bringing in a qualified, experienced expert   to   run   research   correctly   and   without   bias   or   flaws.

UX AND AGILE METHODOLOGIES

"Nobody puts UX in a corner." (Almost a quote from Dirty Dancing)

B uckle your seat belts. I'm going to use SAFe Agile in some of my examples but please know that although a few items are more specific to SAFe, everything here is true for all flavors of Agile and can be adapted to other software development methodologies.

In 2014, I took four days of SAFe Agile training. Yes, I've since recovered. When I asked where UX fits into this model, they told me they had no idea and if I figured it out, I should tell them. *Sigh...*

I've since tried to tell them, but magically, nobody is writing me back. Their lack of cooperation or interest doesn't affect my passion to improve and fix the siloing and disconnecting between UX and other teammates.

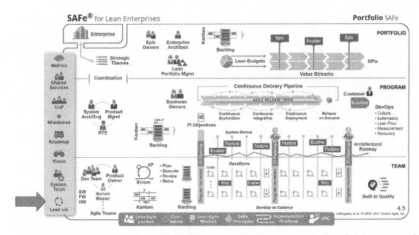

Figure 20: SAFe v4.5. Copyright Scaled Agile Framework. Don't blame me for this. I only added a blue arrow.

UX now gets a little cycle icon on the bottom left in some castaway column, lumped in with milestones, system team, metrics, and other things SAFe appears unsure about. These things aren't related to each other, so this left-side bar must be the junk drawer or island of castaways.

But dropping "Lean UX" on this image doesn't tell me or anybody else how UX works in. **Most Agile books, training, and infographics don't answer questions** like, "What is UX?" "Are UX specialists working in sprints?" "Are they on the team or outside of it?" "How does this affect software development process, estimations, or timeboxing?"

Some people see SAFe's visual and reply, "Well, SAFe is a joke." Maybe or maybe not, but it's hard to find any Agile information or training going deeply into how you work with UX and product designers—the people designing what Engineering will build.

Version 4.5 of the SAFe Agile framework says, "Traditionally, UX design has been an area of specialization. People who have an *eye for design*, a *feel for user interaction*, and *specialty training* were often entirely in charge of the design process." (Emphasis mine, for foreshadowing.)

Is that a problem statement, or are they saying those were the good old days? Yes, putting UX specialists in charge of the design sounds pretty good!

They continue, "The goal was 'pixel perfect' early designs, done in advance of the implementation. Usually, this work was done in silos, apart from the very people who knew the most about the system and its context."

Yes, we need to break down silos and fix collaboration, but otherwise, this also sounds pretty good. We *should* create pixel perfect designs before anybody spends time turning interactions and interfaces into front- or back-end code. What would UX and UI experts deliver to Engineering if we didn't wait until we had tested, finalized designs that were pixel perfect? Something that's sloppy? Unfinished? What dev team wants to work from a non-finalized design that might change later?

Unfortunately, SAFe uses this and other poor reasoning to announce that UX specialists should be removed, because, they claim, that would solve siloing. SAFe's website actually says that they're "empowering Agile teams to do their own Lean UX"... even as companies are learning the value of UX and are moving towards hiring more UX specialists.

SAFe also suggests that you should, "include the design perspectives of Product Management, System Architecture, Business Owners, Information Security, Operations, and Shared Services." It sounds like the Agile team will be doing specialty UX work with everybody at the company except UX specialists. Brilliant! This approach is so bizarre and so far from what is measurably working at companies that it leads one to wonder if someone at SAFe had a very bad romantic breakup with a UX practitioner, and this is revenge.

Where else does your company like to put untrained non-specialists on software development teams? How will that affect productivity and efficiency when Engineering has to take on someone else's job?

And why would untrained non-specialists imagine they can do UX work? Remember the "eye for design" and "feel for user interaction?" These words are carefully chosen to minimize UX experts. You wouldn't say an expert cardiologist just has a "feel" for working with the human heart. You wouldn't say your senior developer sure has an "eye" for working with programming languages. Those people might find those phrases disrespectful.

Those words are there to help Agile team members who self-assess as having "an eye for design" and "a feel for user interaction" decide they are perfectly qualified to do UX work. And when we start talking about self-assessing, we might find ourselves back in Dunning-Kruger and "American Idol auditionee" land.

SAFe appears to believe the *specialty training* isn't really needed as long as you have *eyes* and *feels*.

WHERE UX FITS INTO AGILE

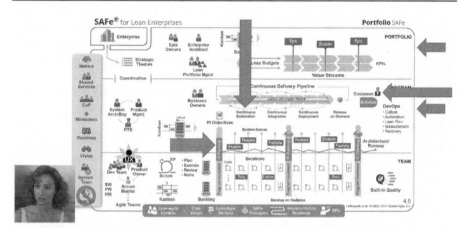

Figure 21: SAFe would have you believe that UX is stuck in a corner with other things they didn't know how to fit in. But UX and Agile are friends.

First of all, nobody puts UX in a corner.

UX should be part of Portfolio, involved in what we're building, why we're building it, and how to make building it a priority.

UX lives in Continuous Exploration, the process of continually exploring the market and user needs, and defining a vision, roadmap, and set of features that address those needs.

We're about Customer Solutions. Completely. It's what we live for.

We're making DevOps better. We want to improve and enhance the culture. We're all about decreasing failure rates, though we're thinking on the human experience level, rather than the technical bug level. We want shorter time between fixes, but we also want there to be fewer fixes.

Better UX design earlier = fewer fixes later.

UX ON THE AGILE TEAM

UX fits into many areas of any flavor of Agile. People who aren't sure where UX fits into Agile mostly don't understand what UX does or why they do it. You're starting to get that now, which makes you the genius hero at your company.

One UX designer should be on the Agile team. They represent the creative team and can circle back with visual designers, copywriters, researchers, and others involved in the larger UX process.

Invite your UX person to standups, retro, release planning, and any meeting or showcase where the UX could be discussed. Don't just showcase UX's work, explain it, or answer for it. Make sure your teammate is there to explain and possibly defend their own work.

If something comes up when UX isn't in a meeting, table that item until you can connect with your practitioner. Missing a meeting isn't an excuse to make decisions in your teammate's field of expertise without them.

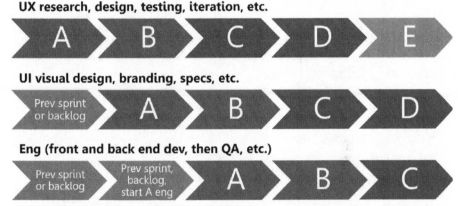

Figure 22: Graphic representation of UX being sprints ahead of Engineering.

To explain the image above, what I have found works best when companies want to work UX into sprints is that UX is at least two or more sprints ahead of Engineering. This gives UX time for its usual processes and tasks including research, design, testing, and iterating.

When the interface and designs are testing well, visual design, branding, iconography, typography, and other aspects of UI can then be applied. Some companies do these as part of their interaction design process. As a non-artist, it's easier for me to separate interaction design and UI, the function from the form. If the designs test poorly, the time spent on UI might be wasted as the interaction designs will need to change and UI redone. Great visual design can't save poor UX and shouldn't mask it. Therefore, I recommend that these processes be separated. Like we don't want Engineering to face cycles of rebuilding or change requests, we don't want artists and visual designers to face cycles of redesigning and change requests as the interaction design evolves.

Therefore, the model I'm suggesting has UI spending a sprint designing what UX passes to them from a previous sprint. If visual designers want to undertake additional testing of their designs, their sprint allots them this time. When UI is done with their process, they can pass full UX blueprints as well as visual design specs to Engineering.

UX should be part of sprints but if the project is new or large, UX must start weeks or months ahead of kickoff—otherwise Engineering won't have something to build. We don't have time machines! We can't kick off today and finish by tomorrow.

Include UX in iteration planning. This means that if work is for an external client, UX should also be part of the scoping and proposal process so that the needed time and budget can be included.

Let UX plan and estimate so that they can get the time they need. Understand that depending upon the features or stories, our work tasks and timing vary greatly. We might just need to wireframe or prototype something quickly. Or this might be something new that requires research and/or testing; in that case, we would need more time to get this ready for dev. This won't be a surprise or delay for anybody if it's properly estimated early on.

Assign tickets to UX when issues, ambiguities, or the like are found during development or QA testing. Whether you use JIRA, Version One, or another system, bring UX into it. Don't leave UX out and don't put UX in some other system like a Trello board if that's not how you track all defects and ambiguities.

Getting a ticket assigned to UX is a *great* way to start the conversation. It also shows respect. You know there is a problem, you know it's a UX problem, and you know you're not going to fix it without your UX specialist. This is a super opportunity for collaboration... but more importantly, it includes UX in the process. Including UX in problem-solving should streamline the workflow and make things more efficient. It's better than a Slack conversation, certainly better than no conversation, and gets the whole process documented.

UX research, design, testing, iteration, etc.

Eng (front and back end dev, then QA, etc.)

Figure 23: If UX runs late and needs more time on "A", Engineering has backlog they can work on.

Get plenty of tech stories or fixing of tech debt into the backlog. If UX's creative and cyclical process runs late, developers can truly be *agile*. Instead of waiting for UX, they can switch to some low-hanging fruit that Product or Engineering has prioritized.

The key to the UX process is user testing *before* delivering anything to Engineering. That way, everyone can be sure this is a great execution of the right idea for our customers. User testing nearly always finds flaws in the design, allowing UX to iterate and improve. Sometimes, there are a surprising number of flaws. It's often best to test again before declaring things finalized.

Things can run late; it happens with Engineering, too. Estimates were off, QA found more bugs than anybody expected, something really broke, oops we need an API call for that, someone called in sick. It happens to the best of us!

And of course, a good UX practitioner or team would keep cross-functional teammates updated so that everybody knows ASAP when things might be or are running late.

WHO ISN'T ON THE TEAM?

Some conference attendees have asked if I'm suggesting that UX should be on the software development team, then who *isn't* on the team? More and more departments are declaring themselves important enough for a spot on the team... so who do you include and who do you exclude? Should specialists in security, systems administration, and other areas that affect Product or Engineering decisions be on the team?

Many models recognize the SME, or Subject Matter Expert. These models indicate that these are people who "consult" with the team but are not on it. I would agree with that model and those boundaries except that UX is often seen as SMEs who are not on the team.

UX experts are specialists and SMEs but they are more than on-demand consultants. UX's work and deliverables are inextricably tied to the whole reason you are building Agile, Scrum, or other types of software development teams. We are designing what you will build, test, and release.

What we have designed is being discussed daily. As developers or QA find ambiguities or have questions, we need to be *right there* to respond quickly. Questions tend to come up about UX designs and decisions in showcases and stakeholder meetings; UX specialists should be there to discuss their own work and choices.

Also remember that UX represents all of Creative including UX specialists, visual designers, copy writers, researches, and others. Your designated UX resource is on the team to represent all of these people most of the time. There are times where these others can be brought in as SMEs more directly. But in many cases, your UX worker speaks for and to everybody falling under the Creative rainbow.

If UX isn't part of the team and we rely on a product manager or product owner to play telephone, we run the risk that people complain that UX isn't available to them. They're siloed. They're not collaborating well enough. Dedication to improved collaboration means bringing UX on to the software dev team.

It's important to draw lines when forming a software development team. Consider giving UX a full-time place at the table rather than seeing them as someone we'll ping here and there, randomly and possibly infrequently.

HIRE THE RIGHT TYPES OF UX SPECIALISTS

Let's say your specialized database programmer is a bottleneck right now... too many stories looking for their specialization. What do you do? Solutions could include pair programming, creating a skills matrix so work can be better balanced in the future, and perhaps you allow more teammates to do exploratory testing so that developers get feedback earlier. Maybe you add another developer to the team.

Do you know what isn't suggested in this scenario? We don't expect that the specialized programmer will teach their specialty to others on the team. I read a Scrum book that warned that UX specialists might be a bottleneck... so they should train other people to do their job.

I studied some BASIC language programming in the 70s, which tells me I have an *eye for programming* and a *feel for coding...* remember those eyes and feels? Would you like to teach me some Ruby because you're backed up with work? Should I go take a 3-day bootcamp and then start coding something that'll go to production?

This doesn't sound like a great solution, does it. Training others to do UX's job hurts productivity, efficiency, product, and culture because UX is being told once again, "Anybody can do your job."

UX research and testing can be a bottleneck. It's frustrating for all of us! Your company will need to hire more of the right people into the UX department so that there are fewer or no bottlenecks. When it comes to staffing, I recommend:

- 1 UX designer or architect can be assigned to up to three projects, depending on project sizes.
- 1 UX researcher supports up to 3 UX architects (and therefore multiple projects).
- If your UX designer or architect is what we call T-shaped, meaning they have some sub-specialties like research and testing, then you might not need specialist researchers, but you'll have to put your UX designer on fewer projects because they'll be taking on more tasks.

REMEMBER AGILE MANIFESTO PRINCIPLES

A few of the Agile Manifesto principles support how you work with UX and product design.

- *Principle 1: Our highest priority is to satisfy the customer.* That's directly linked to how valuable, delightful, easy-to-learn, easy-to-use, and life-improving our product is.
- *Principle 5: Give motivated individuals the environment and support they need and trust them to get the job done.* You have to hire great UX workers, trust them, and give them what they need.
- *Principle 9: Continuous attention to technical excellence and good design enhances agility.* Design matters! Make it GREAT.
- *Principle 10: Simplicity—the art of maximizing the amount of work not done— is essential.* When UX kills or changes features, we're often seen as the bad guys. Engineering should support our efforts to create less work for

everybody by creating fewer or simpler features, or by eliminating projects that are wrong for the company or team to undertake.

Horror Story: Feature With No Customer Value

I was once given a project to rip off a competitor's special shopping filters because the product manager found that 21% of our mobile users weren't filtering search results. I asked him to slice that 21% and show me data that those users don't buy from us, spend less, are unhappy, or can't find what they're looking for. We should only care that they aren't using filters if it's causing a poor customer experience.

I got no response.

I told the team that we shouldn't be building this tool, as it had no customer value. I predicted that the following year's interface simplification project would remove this feature.

The filters were built anyway. They were live on the mobile site. And when the simplification project got to these screens, this feature was removed.

That was six months of a large cross-functional team's time and budget that could have been saved. *Remember simplicity and maximizing the work not done.*

IS UX WATERFALL OR BIG DESIGN UP FRONT?

People who have attended my conference presentations have asked if UX is waterfall. One person told me his company is trying to get away from "Big Design Up Front" (BDUF). He wanted to know why UX wouldn't use fast feedback and iterations.

Of course we use fast feedback and iterations. But let's look at why UX is often mistaken for waterfall or BDUF.

Imagine your company is setting up a new workflow for a customer to sign up and pay for a subscription. The user goes through five steps: creating an account and password, selecting the product, providing payment details, reviewing their order, and completion.

That means that developers can break building this into five chunks... or perhaps into more, even smaller chunks. Engineers have asked me why UX doesn't design step one, deliver that, design step two, deliver that, etc. because that would be "more agile."

Given that UX testing often finds flaws that need to be fixed, if UX were to deliver the first step to Engineering before it completed the entire workflow, how could it test that workflow without potentially asking Engineering for major rebuilds? And if the workflow has flaws, does Engineering want to rebuild what it already coded because it received the designs piecemeal? Do you want to find out after building all five steps that UX only just now tested the whole flow, found that people hate step two, and this process needs to be redesigned by UX and rebuilt by Engineering?

That doesn't sound efficient or like it'll save time, money, or sanity.

Remember that developers can break their work into smaller bits because they know how the story ends. They have stories, features, and the big picture. They can think about all five steps when building step one because they have documentation, information, and blueprints. They might even have wireframes, prototypes, and other UX deliverables that tells them exactly what they're building. Developers shouldn't have to make it up as they go along.

When UX gets a project, we don't know how the story ends. We have vision, ideas, pain points, and innovation concepts. *We have to write the story.* That means that for larger or newer features or products, we can't break our work into small pieces. We don't have the big picture yet. It's our job to create the narrative.

If the project is something smaller than a full user process, of course we can be nimble. We'd do selected tasks or pieces from the UCD process and we'd need less time. Not everything UX does requires a long runway but Product, Project, and Engineering must be prepared when a feature calls for that.

Budgets and timelines are what block UX from getting fast feedback and iterating. There is no expert, experienced UX professional who would volunteer to skip UX research or testing. We always want that feedback, we want to improve, and we want to design what really works for customers. It's not User-Centered Design without users. We don't want to create UX debt, and we don't want Engineering having to fix UX issues later and rebuild, especially when these issues are obvious early on to UX workers and often other teammates as well.

Before complaining that UX is not collecting fast feedback and iterating, check to see whether we were given the budget and timing to collect that fast feedback and iterate on our designs. There's a Grand Canyon between, "Yeah, we're so awesome that we didn't bother testing that," and, "Holy cats, of course we wanted to test that but nobody is letting us!"

Sometimes, you won't be able to get away from Big Design Up Front. UX needs time to cycle through its process. Remember your Agile Manifesto Principles, especially Principle #5: *give motivated individuals the trust and resources they need to do their jobs.* Trust us to work how we need to. We will get this done and the customer will be thrilled. (So will you.)

In an effort to try to streamline processes, I've noticed that non-UX roles sometimes turn necessary elements of UX's approach into some ugly-named, shameful thing "we must get away from." Nobody is campaigning against, "Big

Agile Spike Up Front" because sometimes you need a spike. Please don't decide that any time UX needs a runway ahead of time for a larger project or extra sprints to go through their process that this is some terrible thing that companies must stop doing. It can absolutely fit in when planned appropriately, very early in the process.

UX will always go as fast as they can, but a great UX specialist will do everything they can to avoid sacrificing the quality of the work being done. In the fast versus. good battle, UX will always pick good... and you should too.

AGILE IS "BS" WITHOUT CUSTOMER FEEDBACK

So says the US Department of Defense—seriously. The DOD publicly released an amazing document called, "DIB Guide: Detecting Agile BS." [http://uxui.services/agilebs] (DIB is the "Defense Information Board" and "BS" is an abbreviation for bulls**t.)

I can spend all day telling you that an important part of the software development process is bringing UX specialists in early to make sure that proposed products and features have real customer value, resolve customer pain points, or bring something innovative and desirable.

In addition to the other authors and UX experts who would back me up, here is a flow chart from an October 2018 US Department of Defense document about how to detect BS in Agile. "Agile" has become a buzzword and not every contractor or team promising it to the US military is delivering it. The document offers questions that help determine when a project isn't really Agile and what answers to listen for.

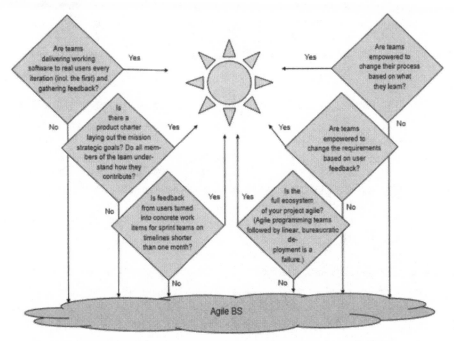

Figure 24: Screen shot of flowchart from the DoD document on detecting BS in Agile.

This graphic may be hard to read but here is the text from some of these fantastic flow chart diamonds, with my commentary:

- **Are teams delivering working software to at least some subset of real users every iteration (including the first) and gathering feedback?** Gathering feedback and designing or iterating based on that feedback must be a part of the process. It's best when UX or CX practitioners or teams handle getting and analyzing feedback.
- **Is feedback from users turned into concrete work items for sprint teams on timelines shorter than one month?** Depending upon what you learn from that feedback, seek to push most fixes out within weeks. Don't make users wait months for an improved experience.
- **Are teams empowered to change the requirements based on user feedback?** This is my favorite one. Based on the feedback of real users, we might need to change requirements, even if that means evolving or scrapping features or entire products. This again highlights the importance of UX collaborating early with product managers, project managers, and anybody in charge of the Agile portfolio. Requirements might need to be changed based on what we know from and about customers. It will save time and money to change those before project kickoff, if possible.

If the answers to any of these is no, you're getting "Agile BS." So says the flow chart!

Sadly, some BS might still get by this flow chart. A military IT worker told me about an outside development contractor her department hired who said they do UX and incorporate user feedback. She said they test what they've built on one user. Based on that, they go and rebuild parts of the system. They then test with another individual. Based on that, they rebuild parts of the system.

This is *not* how UX testing and iterations work. Normally you test with at least five users (separately), gather and interpret the feedback, and then make changes. Sometimes something that one person does or wants doesn't represent the majority or is an outlier. It's important to broaden the testing pool before iterations.

This sounds slow, inefficient, wildly expensive, and appears to be Agile BS *and* UX BS.

COLLABORATING WITH UX

Improve culture and how we work together.

'Ve been in kickoff meetings with people who expected me to have final wireframes two days later because that's how much time they thought it would take. If I need more time, I must surely be trying to derail this project. I was accused of not being "more Lean" or "more Agile." They didn't know about or understand the UX process and they didn't ask. They assumed that drawing boxes on a page is easy and since it should only take a few hours, they're being generous by giving me two days.

UX should be involved in planning (treatments, greybars, however you do it). UX should be present so that we can provide potential timing for our process.

Product managers don't like to hear this, but UX should be involved early in feature ideas just in case the idea isn't a strong one. If Product falls in love with an idea and puts it into the schedule, they expect UX to build it, often without discussion or objection. Product is sometimes closed to hearing why the beloved feature or idea is wrong for the customer. UX is normally told, "Too bad. We planned, we budgeted, we move forward with this project no matter what UX thinks of it."

If Product doesn't have any ego about projects and is dedicated to products and features that are excellent for the customers, and if Product appreciates the Agile Manifesto Principles or being Lean, then Product should welcome UX collaborating early to discuss concepts and features... regardless of the potential outcomes of those discussions.

DON'T PRESCRIBE DESIGNS

Let UX do its job and go through its process. Don't tell us what to build. UX is your best partner when you bring us problems, pain points, and ideas. UX is not really your partner if you are saying, "Hey, here is what company X is doing, make us that."

Horror Story: Don't Prescribe Designs for UX

I once had a product manager email me about a new feature she wanted to get into a treatment. She admitted it was straight off a competitor's website. I asked about the use cases for *our customers*. What problems does this solve for our customers?

She wasn't sure. She asked me if I could think of use cases. I said that I don't want to take a feature off someone else's website and then try to reverse engineer a reason to build it. In UX, we start with real customer pain points or real innovations because those have user stories, and then we go from there.

Why do our customers need it? She wasn't sure.

If you can't come up with good user stories on why customers need this, I'm going to be formally and strongly suggesting that we not build this. Please don't put it in a treatment and ask me later to rip off a competitor.

Her colleagues often sent the UX team completely prescribed work. They were given budget and permission to build this, here are the competitor websites we want to knock off, get us some wireframes.

That's not UX. That's not a creative process. That's not innovation.

DON'T ASK UX TO CREATE DARK PATTERNS

"Dark patterns" are tricks used in product, software, and service design to try to get users to do something they really don't want to do or didn't mean to do. The business usually believes that tricks like these will make them more money, get more conversions, or keep people from cancelling.

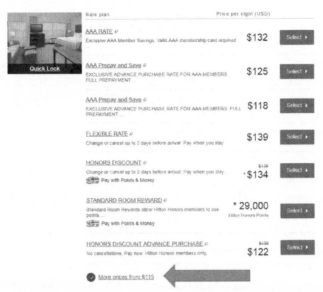

Figure 25: Hotel booking process hides lower prices, hoping you'll pay more.

This image shows prices for a hotel room. Lots of options and some good rates like $125 and $122 per night. What could be slightly evil when they're making so many choices obvious?

Look at the bottom near the giant blue arrow. This hotel offers rates as low as $115 for this night. Why wouldn't they list that lowest rate among the main list? Why hide them under this accordion (expandable section), which people may never notice and never click? They hope you don't book their cheapest rate. It only serves the business to show the customer rates that aren't the lowest without making them jump through a hoop.

It's far from the evilest thing on the internet, but this is something designed deliberately to trick users into paying more. No paying customer would want or prefer an interface that hid the lowest pricing.

Dark patterns are the opposite of User-Centered Design. They put the business completely before the user. Even if you think you have a short- or long-term win for your company, don't insist that your UX partner design something slightly or super evil to achieve that goal. A great UX architect will push back.

DON'T SAY, "WE'LL FIX IT LATER"

Problems rarely get fixed later. Nobody will want to go back and work on it. We have to push ahead to cover more stories, features, and backlog.

Many people know about the Pirates of the Caribbean ride that's at Disney parks around the world. It's roughly a 5-minute boat ride through pirates ransacking a town. If you've been on it, you can't forget the iconic moment your boat moves past the ship firing on El Morro, the Puerto Rican fort.

Would this attraction have been as compelling or fun if it had been a New Orleans-themed walk-through pirate wax museum? That was Disney's original idea and they even started building it. But when Walt saw how popular his new, "It's A Small World," boat ride was, he decided to redesign Pirates to be a boat ride too.

Disney's workers were against it at first. They had already spent time and money building the walk-through museum version. The story goes that Walt didn't care. He wanted to build what people would love the most and that was a boat ride. Undo what you have and start again.

The same is true for your software project. Don't continue building or release something knowing it's broken or not quite right and pretend you'll fix it later. It will cost less to improve this now. Once the public sees it, the cost to change it could be more than time, money, and resources. It could mean a drain on customer service, PR people cleaning up a mess, and social media managers trying to calm people down.

Does this mean you should stop projects at random times because someone thinks they have a better idea? Of course not. People would have loved a walk-through pirate wax museum that had "Disney Magic." They just would have loved a boat ride *more*. This all happened before UX was formalized, but Walt spent a lot of time in the parks watching and listening to people. He counted how many steps they took before throwing garbage on the ground to help him decide how many trashcans to put out. He did things very deliberately and based in real user experiences like UX experts do now.

Building quality in isn't just about technical excellence. It's also about design excellence. A crappy interface that doesn't have engineering bugs is still a crappy interface and likely to cause customer dissatisfaction. We must aim for quality in all areas.

DON'T BAND-AID A BAD IDEA

One hallmark of bad UX is explanation, tutorials, walk-throughs, and tooltips. They tell our customer, "We think or know you will get this wrong. Maybe you're not that bright! But we didn't want to design it better, make it clearer, or care about ease of use. Instead, we will explain what to do and hope you read and understand this."

We all know how much people love to read instructions. More importantly, instructions are a sure sign that our design isn't intuitive or easy to learn and doesn't "just work."

Horror Story: Engineering Overruled UX, Their Idea Failed Testing

I once had an engineering lead tell me in a retail mobile app project that he wanted to remove the shopping cart icon from the top right of the app just for the screens that were part of our particular feature set. And that feature did include people choosing items, putting them in the cart, and then checking out.

He instead wanted a big, red button on the bottom of the screen that said "CHECKOUT." He tried to tell me he wasn't sure people would know to click on the cart icon to start their checkout.

Really?! Then how do they make it through our app as it is currently and has been for years if they don't know what the cart icon means? You want to remove the shopping cart icon, possibly the best-known paradigm on the planet for the last nearly 20 years? Why? He told me it would be "cleaner." The app would be "cleaner" with the shopping cart icon everywhere in the app except our handful of screens?

"Cleaner" normally refers to an interface that lacks clutter (which is good). Did this guy really think the shopping cart icon was cluttering up the app interface? Does he think our shoppers didn't need the cart icon? They seem to need it on every other screen of the entire app.

Mr. Engineering Lead overruled what I had designed to get his way. Then it was built, QA'ed, released, and tested on users in a pilot program. Guess what?

Users who clicked his big, red checkout button thought they had *completed* their checkout in one click. They closed the app and walked away, not noticing that the screen they were taken to was the *cart*, not a confirmation of purchase. Why did customers think that?

When people saw the big red checkout button, they figured: "Aha! I'm logged in, they know my billing info, it must be a one-click checkout like Amazon!" But it wasn't. People hit the checkout button, they thought they were done, and hadn't actually bought anything.

It failed testing. It ran the risk that people using this in a store would be seen as shoplifters for removing items from the store without having actually paid for it. This is a problem! So now what?

Mr. Engineering Genius and his product manager pal came back to me wanting me to fix it. Whew, yes, let's go back to my original design where people will hit the cart icon like they do every other day and go through the checkout like they do every other day. No, they want me to make *their* checkout button idea work. They wanted me to add explanation text like on the next screen telling people, "Now **this** is the checkout screen, you're not done yet."

This is just putting a band-aid on a bad idea. The idea to remove the beloved, clear, and consistent shopping cart icon is a bad idea. Having how you get to checkout be inconsistent around the app is a bad idea. Pushing for your idea to be used even after it failed testing is a bad idea.

Don't ask UX to come up with band-aid solutions that make bad ideas work. There shouldn't be any ego. There should be data, personas, customer feedback, and other gatherable information that helps us know if something is likely to be a great match to customers or not. If a UX pro shoots your idea down, the idea was not the best match to the customer and their needs. And if it fails testing, drop the ego.

When the co-workers in my above horror story saw the testing results, they should not have said, "Hey, that failed. Let's add more things to it until we can say our ideas worked!" They *should* have said, "Oh well, we overruled UX to try our own ideas, our ideas didn't work, let's go back to what the UX expert was recommending." They shouldn't have overruled UX for an ego project that had no data supporting that their ideas were a good match to customers.

It hurts culture and the product for Engineering to overrule UX for a non-engineering reason. If we're limited by technical issues, that's fine. But don't overrule a UX design because you think you have a better idea, you want to put your ego stamp on the project, you really love the way this competitor does something different that you've decided is relevant, or you want to say it's "cleaner" your way. These are bad reasons to unleash poor designs on customers.

UX SAVES THE DAY

There is no longer a good reason or excuse to just build it, just ship it, and then find out later it's a disaster.

I t's not all carnage and disaster. There are plenty of examples of UX saving the day. You can even Google for them; the easiest way to find positive UX examples is to read the case studies on UX testing service and tool websites like UserTesting.com and UserZoom.com. Companies may be more likely to brag about their successes on these sites rather than on their own sites.

Here are three case studies from UserTesting.com.

"It was really valuable to get user feedback early in the prototyping process. That way, we could make changes and find a solution that worked without slowing down our development cycle."

Carol Valdez,
Principal Content Designer
TurboTax

Figure 26: Intuit TurboTax found great value in getting user feedback early in their UX prototyping process. This allowed them to make changes and find solutions without slowing down developers. Screen capture from UserTesting.com.

This first example speaks directly to our DevOps goals. UX wants to iterate before passing off to Engineering... because not following that process might slow Engineering down.

Walmart ⋇

Headquarters: Bentonville, AR
Founded: 1962
Industry: Retail / Ecommerce

Walmart.ca increases on-site conversions by tailoring experiences to customer needs

Fulfills commitment to founding principle, taking a customer-focused approach to digital

Figure 27: Walmart Canada improved workflows and refocused on the customer. They saw a boost to conversions. Screen capture from UserTesting.com.

Walmart Canada's case study also speaks to a goal every company has: a measurable increase in revenue, which they accomplished just from changing page layouts.

One of the reasons we do UX testing before Engineering starts coding is because you love data. In this case study, Walmart declared that numbers are insightful, trackable, and help you trend over time. You can tell stories from numbers. Then blend that with other customer data that CX and UX has.

Walmart saw a 13% increase in revenue just from improving layouts. Walmart doesn't report their Canadian sales separately but they are rumored to be around $25 billion per year in recent years. Depending upon their revenues for the year of this case study, 13% could represent over $2 billion. They did this by doing something that felt simple and natural: taking a customer-focused approach to digital and changing their workflows. I know it's not as simple as it sounds, but this book is your guidebook and map to improving your workflows and processes.

Getting and integrating customer feedback has now become an essential part of the product and engineering team's workflow.

The outcome

With access to study participants and research experts supporting their efforts, the team was able to uncover key insights into how changes in the product were affecting behavior and identify which features were (and weren't) working.

The entire development team—including product managers, designers, and engineers—gathered feedback as often and quickly as needed, in alignment with their rapid development cycle. In fact, UserTesting soon became an integral part of Flipboard's development and release process, allowing the team to make iterative changes to the mobile app based on user reaction.

The team shares the study videos across the organization, helping all team members feel more connected to their users. This in turn helps the team build better products based on a strong understanding of how people use them.

Figure 28: Flipboard found that gathering feedback quickly and iterating worked so well that it's now as essential part of team workflows. Screen capture from UserTesting.com.

Flipboard used UserTesting.com to get customer feedback on how product changes were affecting customer behavior. They were also able to identify which features were and weren't working early in the process without negatively affecting the efficiency of their rapid development cycle. This was such a game changer that they made it part of their standard process. They gathered feedback frequently and quickly.

Even though the case study implies the whole cross-functional team was involved, hopefully they were leaving the actual UX design and UX testing to the UX team, who would then circle back to everybody with the results and interpretations. But certainly, a cross-functional team has many ways to gather feedback that inform what each role does.

No matter which tool or system you use for user testing, there are plenty of case studies describing how companies that added UX tasks, specialists, and testing to their processes are winning.

HIGHLY-PUBLICIZED FAILURES UNDERLINE THE NEED FOR UX SPECIALISTS

In 2018, a Fortune 50 tech company announced it would soon be doing a redesign of last year's redesign. Once the product was released, they found out that customers encountered obstacles, difficulties, and drawbacks in the new features. Customers hadn't asked for these features and they didn't want, need, or like them.

The backlash was serious enough that the company blog admitted the new version was overcomplicated, cluttered, difficult to navigate, and had gone too far with some wacky visual design choices.

How much did this company spend on all of those concepts, layouts, and engineers building and testing it for multiple platforms? How about the cost to undo and redo? One million dollars? Ten million dollars? Think about the time and money this company would have saved if they had pivoted or changed direction before developers wrote a line of code.

UX research helps us understand the target customers so well that UX specialists can tell you early on if an idea or its execution is the right or wrong way to go. UX specialists can also create rapid prototypes of early concepts and run tests on real or archetypal customers to learn if the proposed product design is likely to be a good match.

In 2018, Blizzard's Diablo team got booed at the company's own conference. The headlines said that Blizzard didn't expect fans to be "this angry" about their new mobile game.

If companies do unbiased UX research, they will *not* be surprised by customer reactions after release. If Blizzard had done research, they would have known ahead of time that older customers wouldn't like or use the new version. If they decided to build it anyway hoping to attract new customers, at least they wouldn't have been surprised; they would have made a business decision informed by good data.

Instead, Blizzard was surprised by and unprepared for its customers' reactions to their coming new game. When the company said they were not expecting this degree of backlash, they were admitting they are out of touch with their customers.

We *can* know up front. There is no longer an excuse to just build it, just ship it, and then find out later it's a disaster. Companies can save heaps of time, money, staff resources, and customer agony by integrating the full UX process. Your UX department would have known at multiple points that the proposed new design and features were lacking simplicity, cluttered, and difficult to navigate. Or you were planning a product that old customers will hate and rebel against.

UX specialists should be working hand-in-hand with Product teams early on so that we can block or improve ideas that are unlikely to match the customer.

UX IS A MUST-HAVE AND EASY ON THE BUDGET

With your UX being everything your customer experiences and so central to how they perceive your product and possibly your entire company, who are you trusting with that big of a responsibility?

Despite large public failures and disasters happening at companies of all sizes, many companies are convinced they can't afford UX. Where did bean counters get their budget figures on what UX costs, and how did they decide there wasn't enough of an ROI?

What does incorporating UX practitioners and processes cost?

- UX salaries are often in line with developer salaries, or maybe sometimes a bit higher, but always dependent upon location. For example, in 2018, a Senior UX Designer or a Senior UX Researcher in the San Francisco area might make $125,000, give or take.

- The UX practice requires minimal software, often Sketch and Axure.
- User testing can cost thousands per year, but it's more than worth it and at many companies might be considered a small budget item.

The actual cost for internal company and team changes required for correctly integrating UX practitioners and processes depends how your company approaches changes to process, workflow, and possibly staffing. The costs are mostly around hiring and the training and consulting that teams, departments, and the larger organization would need. Here's how that looks in practice:

- Existing teams, management, and leadership would be trained on new approaches and processes.
- UX specialist managers and leadership would define and formalize:
  o UX strategy
  o UX team values and goals
  o Standardized approaches, tools/software, and deliverables.
- If you have no UX specialists on staff at all, you'll need to hire. Whether you bring in freelancers, contractors, full-time employees, or an outside agency, hiring tasks include:
  o Writing job descriptions.
  o Assessing candidates and their portfolios.
  o Selecting talented people who are great culture fits and will *not* be short order cooks (or treated as such).
  o Onboarding and training new workers.
- A customized, actionable, and concrete plan on what projects, processes, and workflows will look like with the new (or renewed) focus on the user experience including the User-Centered Design process.

Luckily, most of these are things you can put in place and leave unchanged probably for a few years.

When I give people that list, they often feel overwhelmed. They have no idea how to start or approach any of these, especially when UX isn't part of their organization at all. This is where expert trainers and consultants are important, if not necessary.

For those still imagining that UX is expensive and possibly not worth it, compare what your company might spend on UX to:

- Having to add more customer service reps because people find the new features or the product itself frustrating, confusing, disappointing, cluttered, or difficult.

- Throwing more money at your social media managers to handle the complaints launched at online.
- The cost of employees who leave because creating customer dissatisfaction is soul-crushing.
  - Knowledge out the door.
  - Cost to recruit, onboard, and train.
  - Loss of productivity during this transition.
  - Morale and culture impact when co-workers see teammates quitting and wonder or know why.
- Increasing marketing spend because this *piece of junk* is hard to sell or you're trying to win back customers who left.
- Having Engineering rebuild when customer backlash forces product changes.
- Explaining to shareholders or the board why you're bleeding customers, your profits sank, or the stock just dropped.
- Offering discounts on your product because you're struggling to compete against companies who invested in user experience pros.

MEASURING RESULTS

UX wants to know why, not just what or how many.

ithout customer satisfaction, you might not have customers.
If you like quantitative data, we can measure how improving your processes by integrating UX has made positive changes. But we must look beyond the typical software development metrics of productivity, efficiency, or velocity. None of those will matter if you are continuously deploying junk. All teams should have access to and should be reviewing metrics and qualitative data from the voice of the customer.

Look at data from customer service, your call center, and your social media accounts. You are looking for:

- Fewer complaints
- Better app reviews, higher app ratings
- Fewer support tickets
- Fewer call center calls
- More positive sentiment in social media posts

Checking other metrics, you might find:

- More app installs or fewer uninstalls
- Increased AOV (average order value)
- Higher conversion rate

Our desired DevOps results are measurable as well. How long do stories, projects, and epics take to get to market before and after your UX revolution? Developer time estimates should become more accurate when Engineering has finalized UX designs on which to base their estimates, as opposed to working from stories or whatever you're doing now.

If UX is providing blueprints and those are being followed, Engineering should have less work because UX reduced surprise changes and rebuilds.

Internal communication and changes to culture are measurable, but mostly through qualitative or anecdotal means. If you prefer numerical data, then run surveys with your workers. Ask them to rate experiences such as:

- Are you having fewer conflicts with UX or on cross-functional teams?
- Are people collaborating and communicating better?
- How is your productivity and efficiency? (While you can measure that without a survey, how people perceive it is also important as it might speak to how they feel about their jobs.)

WHEN IT GETS WORSE BEFORE IT GETS BETTER

When you are making organizational and process changes, you might see things get worse before they get better. If metrics show a decline in things you expected to improve, what might be going wrong?

- Are we building the *right* product and features? We will not make customers happy or happier without building more of the right software.
- Is Product collaborating with UX on what features, stories, or products to build?
- Are we allowing UX to kill or alter ideas during initial planning and treatments?
- Is UX being overruled, circumvented, or excluded? Empower and include UX. Don't let others do their specialized job.
- Make sure you allot time and budget for user testing. This can help you know before developers build whether or not the idea and execution are poor.
- Quality, experience, and expertise of UX practitioner(s). Who is doing the UX work? Juniors? Artists? Non-specialists? Non-UX roles?

If you haven't made enough changes or the right changes in the above areas, take another pass at further improvement before declaring any failure.

Continue working with UX throughout development and after release. Some companies treat UX like our process is done once the software, system, or feature is released. We'd prefer to stay on the project or at least stay in touch with someone, perhaps a CX specialist, who is collecting and analyzing data after the release.

UX wants to iterate. It's not enough to just see the collected data. UX would want to then work with Product to get stories into the backlog or other projects spun up. For many UX pros, an interface is never really done. The customer is constantly changing. Technology changes. Products and features change. The competition is changing. UX has to stay on top of how users connect or disconnect with the products and services so we can continually improve them.

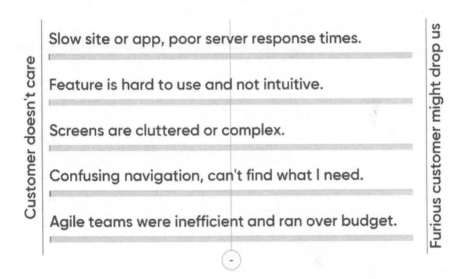

Figure 29: A poll I give presentation attendees asking them to rate how likely certain issues are to drive customers away.

At live versions of my DevOps ICU program, this is one of the live polls attendees to fill out. Each item is rated on a scale from: "Customer doesn't care," on the far left to: "Furious customer might drop us," on the far right. Visit https://menti.com and use code 187448. Find the question asking: "How bad are these problems for our customers?" and vote.

Time after time, each audience rates the first four fairly high, an average score of around eight out of 10. The last one usually averages around a two out of 10.

The first four deeply affect the user's experience, their perception of your software, and their perception of your company. The last one about timing and budget is certainly bad news for DevOps, and maybe the customer has to wait a little longer for the next release, but internal processes going poorly might not affect the customer.

This poll clearly demonstrates to those voting that poor UX is enough to make customers leave or consider leaving. Which means it's important. UX is make or break.

Consider the poll question about how customers are affected by site or system speed and performance. In the past, customers separated a good website or system from server issues or technical choices that made the site slow. "This website is slow, but it's good."

However, site and app performance are being increasingly perceived by the customer as part of the user experience. Instead of excusing a slow system, they will be more likely to find slow response times frustrating and a deal-breaker... and they might drop you.

That means that fixing server issues, refactoring, and immediately addressing database issues should move to the top of everybody's to do list. Being slow had no positive qualities to begin with. As people become less patient, slowness in any of the following areas will really kill the customer experience:

- First Contentful Paint – How long it takes for the first text and images to load.
- First Meaningful Paint – How long it takes for the primary content of the page to be visible. The user can now see some or all of the page, but often can't use it yet as important elements and code are still loading.
- Time to Interactive – How long it takes the page to be fully interactive. Have you ever tried clicking on things while a page was loading and nothing seemed to work? You were stuck in the limbo between the early paints and TTI.
- First CPU Idle – How long it takes until everything has loaded and the page is now ready to handle user input.
- Search Results – We all hate slow search results, poor metadata, or anything else that lowers the quality of the search experience.
- Other dynamic in-page or on-screen data or results - How long do users want to see a spinner while they wait for something to happen? They don't want to see one at all. We now expect everything to be instantaneous. How fast can your teams make your site and databases?

IMPROVE COLLABORATION AND CULTURE

Foster mutual respect and collaboration.

Can you imagine your Engineering department having a meeting and saying, "OK, we need to figure out how to explain to executives that programming, hiring good programmers, and giving us the time and tools programmers need are all really important. How are we going to explain this to our execs? We really need to evangelize engineering."

That's not a thing, right? Yet, this is what UX workers feel like they have to do daily. It makes them look weird and whiny. It looks like a cry for help... and it might be. The help is that UX is so often misunderstood that it feels the need to explain everything in this book (and more) to teammates, stakeholders, managers, and executives.

Horror Story: "UX is Lean Waste!"

I once had a Lean Triad engineering guy openly laughing at me in meetings and cheering his programmers when they ignored and excluded UX, choosing to "design" things themselves. He was gleeful because he was sure that engineers circumventing UX and designing their own concepts without collaboration was *really Lean*.

He howled to a stunned meeting room, "UX is Lean waste!" and declared that he celebrated his programmers eliminating this "waste."

You know who stood up to him and stood up for me? Nobody. The room was silent. People just looked around at each other. There had to be 20 people in that room that day, all from different disciplines.

I tracked him down a year later and sent him a message on LinkedIn. I wanted

---

> to interview him about why he feels that UX is Lean Waste. He told me I got him all wrong! He knows how important UX is! He suggested I read more books about Lean.
>
> Ah, it must be me. Again.

Managers and leaders, inspire respect between your workers. You need to collaborate with other teams and department heads to make sure this is top-down. If workers are being respectful but leaders are disrespectful, you are making it a more negative workplace. You are making it harder for UX to do its job. You are helping to create a worse product for customers by trying to bypass what UX does.

UX isn't waste. UX isn't derailing your projects. UX isn't a black box. We must create and encourage a culture of mutual respect. If that's not coming from the top down, then you start it, bottom up. Don't assume nobody cares, and don't settle for, "Well, we've always done it this way without these UX people so we must not really need them."

Talk to managers and leadership about what you've learned here about how productivity, efficiency, collaboration, culture, product, and customer satisfaction can be improved.

If you're a coach, trainer, or consultant, teach people about UX specialists and tasks. Specifically mention UX as part of the team and culture.

Nobody would stand for manual or automated QA testing being circumvented because, "Our developers write great code and we don't need to test their code before releasing it to the public." Everybody's job is important. Everybody should be empowered to do their job and to be respected for what they bring to the process.

It takes everybody to be part of a culture that fosters mutual respect.

SHOULD EVERYBODY ON THE AGILE TEAM BE AN EXPERT UX DESIGNER?

A mailing list email described a featured video as follows:

> *"The design of a delightful customer experience doesn't come from a single person, nor does it come from a singular role or job title within a company. How do we drop the "rock star designer" attitude, drive shared understanding, embrace an inclusive and diverse process, and*

> *make it our goal to help everyone become as excellent of a designer as they can be?"*

Does the person who wrote this also have a goal of improving inclusivity and diversity, dropping the "engineering rock star attitude," and helping product managers, project managers, business analysts, visual designers, and user experience pros become *as excellent of a developer as they can be*?

"How do we make it our goal to help everybody be a great or better designer?" **That shouldn't be a goal.** UX is a specialty and requires natural talents, skills, studies, and approaches. It's a craft where people level up over time. Nobody graduates from a bootcamp, trade school, or college and is automatically an expert at the top of their game. The same is true for developers.

Additionally, trying to teach non-UX roles to do UX work and spending time (and possibly training budgets) trying to make "everybody" a better designer raises questions that the people proposing these methodologies magically never seem to address, including:

- How are engineering's productivity and efficiency improved when engineers spend time trying to be a better product designer?
- Is UX work the best way for specialist developers and QA to spend their time? Do your engineers have too much free time that nobody knows how to fill?
- Will you improve your Engineering velocity if your engineers have to devote some of their time to UX tasks? Will Engineering get to more or fewer story points while trying to also do my job?
- Where does the slippery slope end? Should engineers work on being better graphic designers? Illustrators? Should engineering spend time learning product management? Is there any role engineers *shouldn't* try to learn or do?
- What kind of culture are you creating when you don't want me to do your job but you want to do mine (and we're equally unqualified to do each other's jobs)?
- If you wouldn't want me coding something that'll go to production, why do you imagine I will want you to do specialized UX tasks?

Yes, I can be a bit grumpy about it, sorry. But I believe it's evolving and improves every month. More and more people are realizing, "Hey wait, we don't do this to other roles," or, "Yikes, letting the programmers design our products hasn't been working for us. Maybe we should hire those specialists we keep hearing about."

We also saw Silicon Valley VCs go from saying that you need great developers to saying that good programmers are a dime a dozen, and you really need amazing UX. How many startups have failed because of product-market fit (a UX issue) versus how many failed because they didn't hire better developers?

Back to the above quote about the video that will discuss ending the "rock star designer attitude," notice that the quote contains the buzzwords "inclusive" and "diverse." These are there to trick you into believing that if the UX team doesn't want to "help everybody" become "excellent designers," then they're not being inclusive or diverse. This is surreal because a company's creative team is often the most inclusive, diverse, high empathy, collaborative, and groovy bunch of people you have in your organization.

Sounds like we're moving the goalposts here. Someone assumes that we high-empathy UX practitioners will have an emotional reaction to being accused of not being inclusive or diverse... and these accusations will make us want to *prove* we are by helping you get better at *our* jobs.

No true UX practitioner will fall for that. Call me a rock star, say I'm not inclusive, not diverse, call me yucky and mean, tell me I have a bad attitude, and tease me that nobody will sit with me at lunch. I won't be manipulated by name-calling. I'm not impressed by that tactic and you're not catching any flies with that honey.

If you would like to be the most excellent designer you can be, put in the work UX pros have put in to get where they are. Complete a two-year master's degree in Human-Computer Interface, Interaction Design, UX Research, or the like. Spend years working at different companies and leveling up your craft and approach.

Let's rewrite that featured video description and make it what someone who cares about customer experiences, inclusivity, and diversity would have written:

> *"The design of delightful customer experiences comes from one role, team, or department at your company - user experience. It's their name! How do we drive UX understanding, embrace inclusivity by respecting UX specialists and integrating them, welcome the diversity of an expert UX designer role onto the software development team, and make it a goal to improve collaboration, communication, and culture?"*

OK, I think we fixed it!

Take it from Phil Gilbert, General Manager of IBM Design. He knows it doesn't make sense to try to turn everybody into a designer.

> *"Not everyone is a designer, but everybody has to have the user as their north star. Day-to day collaboration between engineering and design is the only way to get thoughtful designs into final release in an agile fashion."*
> *– Phil Gilbert, General Manager of IBM Design*

ROCK STAR ISN'T AN INSULT

The people who want to make it a goal for everybody to become great at product designer sound like more people misunderstanding UX. They sound like SAFe announcing that the solution to collaboration issues and siloing is to deny UX its role or specialty.

We each do our best work for our customers when we find ways to come together as a team and play to each role's strengths.

But let's talk about rock stars. We call people rock stars when they are getting it right. They're successful. Most of them have unique, rare, or unmatched talent. They are making their fans (their customers) very happy. They're making everybody money. They're role models —idolized— and are literally hung up on posters. It sounds pretty good to be a rock star. Everybody wants to be a rock star.

The biggest music stars on our planet didn't get where they are alone. The best rock stars have a great band behind them. They have song co-writers. They have agents. The rock star has her success thanks to great collaborations and partnerships. The rock star is doing most of the heavy lifting but it's a team effort. Just like our work teams.

That rock star attitude might just be confidence. Expert UX practitioners come to the table without ego and hope others do the same. Learn to see the rock star in each team member, to appreciate their specialties and talents. Each person plays an important role and each person shines at a different time.

If you can follow my advice and correctly integrate UX practitioners and processes into software development teams, the fans will be happy, everybody will be making money, and I promise it'll all work out. Someone might even hang a poster of your rock star self on their wall... and not be throwing darts at it.

WHO CAN WE BLAME?

Some engineers and product managers have told me that all of the bad blood between UX and non-UX roles is UX's fault. The most common complaints include:

- UX acts like dedicated specialists who aren't part of the team.
- Silos, silos, silos.
- UX is a black box killing our timing!
- UX disappears for weeks or months without a word and then delivers something we're just supposed to build.
- Our Agile training didn't say anything about how to work with UX so they must be unimportant, replaceable, or expendable.

These *sound* like valid complaints, especially the ones about timing. A project manager who gave me two days for a task that takes weeks or longer told me I'm a "non-team player who tries to derail projects" because I wanted more than two days. But UX's style, approach, or agenda is not to derail projects.

UX wants the best product for customers over anything else. If we had data proving that processes went better, product was improved, and customers were happier when developers, QA, and other non-UX roles did UX tasks, we'd be all over it. We'd be hounding you at your desk wanting to teach you more UX principles.

Except that's not what's happened. We've found that everything works better when UX specialists do the UX work, and others stick to their own specialized and important roles. Please notice that only non-UX workers are announcing methodologies and approaches that exclude, minimize, or dilute UX. And the only UX workers who would agree with these methodologies are impostors.

You've heard some of my stories of being misunderstood, belittled, circumvented, overruled, and excluded by Engineering and Product. These stories are all from the 2010's, rather recent. I'm a high-level practitioner with over 20 years in UX and extensive Agile training and experience. I love collaboration, I want to hear ideas and feedback, I'm a friend to developers, and considering I'm teaching this, I certainly know all the "UX plus software dev" best practices.

If this unpleasantness is happening to me, you can be sure that UX practitioners at all levels, especially those junior to me, face stories like mine and worse weekly, possibly daily.

Put on your empathy hat and imagine what people think and say about UX... being thought and said about your job. What would *you* do? Would you be in a big rush to join that team's meetings and talk about your work? Would you like to ask people who think that little of you for feedback on what you've built? Here comes another day of standing in front of a firing squad.

So instead, UX workers sometimes choose to avoid engineers and silo themselves, thinking that if we can't play nicely together, we will just play separately. It's a cycle; departments and teams are disconnecting more and more because they see more and more disconnection. It isn't right and it isn't working.

We can point fingers at UX to collaborate more, but they can't unilaterally fix a process, culture, and the obstacles other teammates and departments put up. That's like looking at an unhappily married couple and expecting one person to fix all of the problems.

This is a two-way street but I'm talking to you because from what you've learned about UX even from this book, you know that great UX specialists are curious, lack ego, like to test, get feedback, and iterate. They want to build the best product for the customers no matter who had that best idea. Their nature is to be collaborative, including Product and Engineering in certain parts of the process.

But the UX practitioners who are great collaborators and friends to Engineering and Product are often not getting a chance when placed on teams with people who think UX *just draws boxes on a page, only needs a few hours at most to produce a completely finalized interaction design*, and can be excluded if the engineering lead or product manager has an idea they like better.

"WE TRIED 'DOING UX' AND IT DIDN'T WORK"

At many companies, someone leads efforts to try one or more of the bizarre approaches I've mentioned, including:

- Following SAFe's idea to remove UX specialists.
- Insisting that UX practitioners train others to do their job or *help make everybody the most excellent designer they can be.*
- Hiring artists to do UX.
- Hiring short order cooks when you really needed creative interface scientists.
- Sending non-UX roles to a conference session, boot camp, or to read some UX books (so they can do UX tasks).
- Giving UX work to "anybody" because UX is easy and anybody can do it.

Companies try these things and when the UX is poor and the customers react negatively, what do they say? "We tried UX and it really didn't work for us. It's not worth the investment."

Unfortunately, whatever you did wouldn't qualify as UX to any UX expert.

But the non-UX workers read the UX book, heard the conference session, or took the boot camp! What could have gone wrong? Those workers are as good at UX as I would be after reading a book on coding, listening to a conference session, or taking a dev boot camp. I wouldn't meet your company's standards, would I?

Or you hired a "UX person" who was really an artist, someone with a very visual and impressive portfolio. Without knowing *how* to hire for UX, you might not have hired someone who was truly a specialist or expert in User-Centered Design.

That means it's time to try again, but this time, you need to do it correctly. If you are not properly and thoroughly integrating UX specialists and the User-Centered Design process, please don't tell yourself your team "did UX."

Chances are when your company wanted to transition into Agile, you got training. You probably didn't have one person on the team read one book or take a conference session and then everybody decided boom, teams were now Agile. You might have gone for training, brought someone in for corporate training, or had a consultant lead you through the transformation.

IT'S A TWO-WAY STREET THAT NEEDS REPAVING

It's time to rewrite the book. Refresh any poor or incomplete training.

UX specialists are as important to your organization as your expert product managers, engineers, and other roles. This means we should no longer give UX work to the cheapest person who claims to be able to make wireframes.

Work with UX leadership on improving collaboration, culture, tools, workflows, and processes. If your company does not yet have UX leadership, you should be hiring for it. But for now, collaborate with senior-level or higher UX practitioners at your company - even if they are freelancers or contractors – to outline and formalize UX strategy.

If none of those apply to you because you have zero UX workers at any level, then connect with an agency or consultant who can work with you on creating a strategy that includes integrating UX roles, processes, documentation, and leadership.

It's time to stop pointing fingers. It doesn't matter how we got here. It only matters that everybody involved is doing their part to pave some new roads. The path to getting your DevOps out of the ICU and seeing improved DevOps results, great product, and happy customers is the complete and correct integration of UX specialists and processes.

DESCRIBE UX IN THREE WORDS

Visit https://menti.com and use code 187448. Find the question asking you to choose three words to describe UX and add them to our word cloud.

EXERCISES

Want to try some of the things you've learned about? Great! Let's do some exercises.

CUSTOMER JOURNEY MAP

Part of UX research is often creating a customer journey map. A customer journey map looks at the customer's process, step by step, stage by stage. As she goes through each step, what does she do, how does she do it, and how does she feel about it?

By including thoughts and emotions, we can also identify pain points. Where does she struggle or hit a wall? Where could her process be faster, easier, or more intuitive?

A journey map isn't a flow chart. It's a visual walk through the emotional highs and lows of what your customer might be doing now with your product or with a competitor's. Perhaps it's her process of shopping for a vendor or item.

A good customer journey map will tell a detailed story from the customer's perspective. It is most often presented as a linear journey but is sometimes shown as a repeating cycle if that's appropriate to the customer's experience.

The map can help settle arguments in a cross-functional team because it forces you away from the mirror and into the mindset of the customer. Put that empathy hat on again!

Here's an example of what it might look like when a customer tries to book a hotel room because they are attending an event or conference. We're using Robyn as our persona and we're imagining the company creating this map is a hotel chain looking to better understand the customer experience.

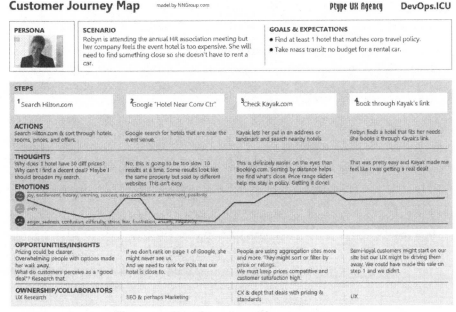

Figure 30: Sample customer journey map

That's a little hard to read. So here is a URL from which you can download the three documents you'll need for this exercise, including the doc you see in Figure 30 above. [https://devops.icu/map-exercise/] It's a ZIP file with three PNG files: the above sample customer journey map, a blank one, and our Carrie persona from earlier in the book.

Now think about Carrie's journey to shop for insurance. Pick any type of insurance she might need... auto, long term care, renter's insurance, anything. What are her steps? What are her actions and thoughts as well as moments of fear, happiness, excitement, or confusion? Map it out!

Download the docs here and give it a try! Watch out for moments where you are writing *your* journey versus the one Carrie would be on.

INFORMATION ARCHITECTURE - TREE TEST

A tree test is done by UX to make sure that a proposed structure and navigation for a website, app, or system makes sense to the user.

The test you'll take reproduces the Apple.com sitemap from their Latin America site, which is way smaller than their USA site, so it's easier for us to test quickly. You'll get some tasks that ask you where you'd find things. And we can determine if our proposed navigation is going to be a winner for customers.

https://devops.icu/treetest/

This is a test that UX gives to customers so it's not part of your job to create this test, take the test, or interpret the test. But you'll be more familiar with UX tasks if you try this out yourself.

You are reading a book and not here with me live, so sadly, I can't then talk to you about the results from the test. But take a look at how easy or hard it was to find things around the Latin American Apple.com website featured in our tree test. Did you have to backtrack and try another path to feel confident you completed the task? Were there times you felt like it was a trick question and what I was asking you to find didn't even exist? They all exist, I promise!

One reminder: a menu that says "more" or "miscellaneous" often isn't clear or helpful to people. That's not part of a logical hierarchy. That list usually contains the items that fall into the, "We didn't know where else to put this," bucket. Good IA knows where to put everything.

Sneaky trick of this test: most of the items you're looking for aren't where you think they are. They're where Apple put them but they might not be where you're expecting them. You are likely to "fail" the test. That doesn't mean you did poorly or this is your fault. A tree test with failures should inspire the internal team to rethink their hierarchy or organization so that it's easier for people to find things.

RATE THE CUSTOMER VALUE AND BUSINESS VALUE OF AN IDEA

Visit https://menti.com and use code 187448. There are three poll questions asking you to rate whether an idea is good or bad for the business, and good or bad for customers. This exercise helps you consider customer value, valuing the customer over the business, and why UX sometimes wants to kill or change features, stories, or projects.

To take these polls, you'll need some background information. Review the background info here in the book (coming up next) and then go to the poll and vote. My answers for each are under the pictures, so don't scroll and read more until you considered each one and cast your vote.

Home screen announcement... good or bad UX?

Imagine you open up a mobile app and in addition to the usual home screen messages, marketing, and whatever it has, you also have a module telling you what's not working today.

The argument I heard in favor of this was hey, we should tell people up front what's broken. That way, they don't try to do the broken things. It's helpful to the user and therefore we should build this.

Right now our site registration is down but login is working.

Search is working but slowly.

Figure 31: Home screen announcement of what's not working.

At a company that had technical issues nearly daily, this is a bad idea. First, I may not be here to interact with the broken areas. If registration isn't working but I'm registered and logged in, I'll never experience this problem.

Second, this may end up giving people the impression that our app and systems are buggy. If they feel like they are seeing these messages often, no matter what they say, we will give people the impression that this app doesn't work well or often. This is where cognitive psych comes into play. What are we teaching or training people to think about this company if they see error messages some or all of the time they go into our app? Will that chip away at trust?

The better solution is to message these things when people get to that area or screen. If someone tries to register right now, sorry, this portion of our app is under maintenance. Please try again and give a time when it's likely to be fixed. Or give us your email and we'll notify you when it's working again. How's that for service!

Order of shoe sizes

Who benefits when shoe sizes are shown in order of how many styles you have available instead of in order of size? The argument for this came from a data person who said that customers would want to know which shoe styles have the most of a certain size available. Shoes might be seen in the orders you see here, each shoe being organized differently. Sizes would also change order every time you loaded an item since stock would change.

Sizes 9, 7, 8.5, 7.5, 10, 6, 7.5, 6.5, 8, 9.5

Sizes 8.5, 9, 6, 7.5, 6.5, 10, 9.5, 8, 7

Figure 32: Shoe sizes in varying orders.

I wear a size 9.5. If you have more styles in an 8, I can't get an 8. So it's nice that you have that but it doesn't help me. I can only see what you have in my size.

I would say this is a poor idea and it doesn't benefit the user or the business. The user definitely loses when sizes aren't in size order and has to think and search and scan for her size. The user loses when every shoe has sizes listed in a different order since the stock will be different in that shoe. And the business gains nothing by showing shoes in this order. So this is an all-around bad idea.

Deleted Facebook account live for two weeks

I deleted my personal Facebook account. I had a separate biz account that rarely posts and has nearly no friends because a business group I was in insisted on using Facebook groups.

I was told that deleting my personal account was successful and that I had 30 days to change my mind. That's fair.

But when I visited my personal Facebook account from my biz account, I found the account totally live. Anybody could see all the posts and pictures. You could even like, comment, and tag me. My personal account was live for 2 solid weeks – without me logging in, using it at all, or reactivating it - before it dropped off the Facebook system.

Figure 33: Deleted Facebook account is still live.

This a bad idea. The user wants to delete her account. She expects that her account is now off Facebook, which might be especially important if her safety has been threatened from other Facebook users.

But it benefits Facebook to not really delete the account. Facebook wants to show active accounts, especially if it needs people to see ads. So it will create an account shutdown that doesn't really shut down the account.

This is also a dark pattern and a bit of bullying. Facebook does this so that people will interact with your account and then reach out to you to say: "Hey, I'm writing to you on Facebook and you're not responding!" You will feel like, "Ugh, I guess I have to be there. People are looking for me."

If a user wants to delete, upgrade, downgrade, etc. you can give them options but ultimately you let them do it. Don't make it mysterious or creepy.

OK, NOW WHAT?

This book is pretty close to the 120-min version of my DevOps ICU workshop if you do the exercises and interactive polls. Congrats, you made it through! Where can you go from here?

LET'S CONNECT

- https://DevOpsICU.com/ is the website for this training program. I offer:
  - Private, in-person corporate trainings.
  - Partnerships with Agile, business transformation, and engineering consultants, trainers, and coaches. You're probably not teaching any of the material I'm teaching. And you're probably not a UX expert, so it would be hard for you to take spontaneous questions. That's where partnering makes much more sense!

- https://pty.pe is my UX agency. We can help with:
  - UX projects.
  - Augmenting your existing UX team, coming in as freelancers, contractors, or an outside agency.
  - Providing on-call UX leadership. Great for companies who started with a small team or one UX practitioner but hired juniors. They need mentoring, soft skills, work reviews, escalations, and other help. We can act as your on-call UX leadership.
  - Building or improving your internal UX team or practice. Creating values, standards, writing job descriptions, assessing

candidates, hiring, selecting management, choosing tools and software, working with other departments on how to integrate UX, etc. We can customize our private consulting for anything you need.

- https://DebbieLevitt.com is my website for my speaking and writing. If you have an internal or public event seeking a qualified, fun, and information-packed speaker or corporate trainer, hey, that's me!

- https://www.linkedin.com/in/debbielevitt/ Find me on LinkedIn and send a connection request. I typically don't accept people who don't write a little note, so please include a note saying you read the book so I know you're not a creepy salesperson.

- https://pty.pe/cal is my online appointment system. Want to talk to me? Book some time, no charge. The system will send you a conference call/screen share.

- Hate shuffling through websites? Just email me at DEB@PTYPEUX.COM.

SPECIAL THANKS TO MY EDITORS

Piles of gratitude to the friends and colleagues who helped me with my DevOps ICU training program and/or this book. Get to know them! Hire them as speakers, leaders, or whatever they're doing now!

In no particular order:

- Atul Damani [linkedin.com/in/adamani]
- Lee McLoughlin [linkedin.com/in/leemcl]
- Arash Matinrazm [linkedin.com/in/matinrazm]
- Jill Ivey @ https://www.jilletante.com
- Travis [linkedin.com/in/travis-j-bjorklund/]
- Angela [linkedin.com/in/angela-prentner-smith/]
- Evan Daly [linkedin.com/in/evan-daly]
- Ira Wolfe [linkedin.com/in/irawolfe]
- Chris Lenhart [linkedin.com/in/chrislenhart72]
- Shann Bossaller [linkedin.com/in/shannb/]

Without these people, the DevOps ICU training program, conference session, workshop, and book wouldn't be as great as they now are. I'm very grateful for their time, conversations, editing, and in some cases, tough love.

Made in the USA
San Bernardino, CA
17 April 2019